Christopher's Journey

To my friends at The Community Foundation, I love your _journey_ with our community! ♡

[signature]

Contents

PREFACE. ix

FOREWORD. xi

INTRODUCTION xiii

Part I　　　*CHRIS'S FIRST PROTOCOL: 1997–1998*

CHAPTER 1　　A DANGEROUS DIAGNOSIS. 3

CHAPTER 2　　THE QUEST FOR REMISSION 16

CHAPTER 3　　LIFE IN TREATMENT. .23

CHAPTER 4　　WHAT ANGELS ARE MADE OF 35

CHAPTER 5　　A TRUE FRIEND 45

CHAPTER 6　　THE END OF INPATIENT 50

Part II　　　*REMISSION: 1998–1999*

CHAPTER 7　　THE GIFT OF REMISSION. 59

CHAPTER 8　　FAMILY 78

Part III　　*CHRIS'S SECOND PROTOCOL: 2000–2001*

CHAPTER 9　　RELAPSE 93

CHAPTER 10　　AN UNCERTAIN FUTURE. 102

CHAPTER 11　　LIVING IN THE MOMENT 118

CHAPTER 12   A SPECIAL FAMILY 124

CHAPTER 13   LAUGHTER AND TEARS 128

CHAPTER 14   ARE WE REALLY DONE? 135

CHAPTER 15   SHORT-LIVED REMISSION 140

Part IV   *THE END OF THE JOURNEY: MARCH 2001–JULY 2001*

CHAPTER 16   THE MONSTER RETURNS 145

CHAPTER 17   THE COMMUNITY REACHES OUT 152

CHAPTER 18   DEVASTATION 160

CHAPTER 19   CHRIS'S GOLDEN HOURS 168

CHAPTER 20   BEAUTY AND PAIN 177

CHAPTER 21   A FEATHER UNDER MY PILLOW 181

EPILOGUE: LETTERS TO CHRIS 183

Acknowledgments

A special thank-you to my good friend and editor, Barbara Mistichelli: you waded through my first draft, dispelled my random acts of comma, and provided a continuous dialogue of love and encouragement

To Dr. Jerry Barbosa who did everything humanly possible to help our Christopher, and when you could do no more healing, you graciously donated your time and talent to provide medical input during the editing process.

To Bob, my husband, and Christopher's dad: thank you for sharing this journey with me, and for being a computer widower for many long months.

PREFACE

Christopher's Journey began as a notebook that I used to record the overwhelming flood of medical information that accompanies a cancer diagnosis. Finding myself suddenly immersed in the new and terrifying world of pediatric cancer, I also became acquainted with many dedicated professionals and caring volunteers. They were soon added to my log. Finally, there were the personal aspects of the experience—the tremendous emotional upheavals, the spiritual searching, and the impact that the disease has had on Chris and all of us who love him.

During the four years of Chris's treatments the journal became my therapy, my textbook, and my way to recount the many inspirational conversations with my son. That first notebook eventually grew to four, one for each year of Chris's treatment. After Chris's passing, I began publishing short magazine articles, but my heart and soul always wandered back to those original tear-stained notebooks.

Finally, after several years of writing and revising, *Christopher's Journey* emerged. Thanks to the medical expertise of Dr. Jerry Barbosa, who assisted with the technical editing of *Christopher's Journey*, the book accurately explains the details in the treatment of a young leukemia patient. But Christopher's journey has been so much more than physical. It has been mental, emotional, and spiritual as well. In portraying those nonmedical aspects of the journey I drew upon my greatest resource—a mother's heart.

Foreword

By Al Bogutz

Serenity. Adults seek it in organized religion, the arms of a lover, possessions, career, and chemicals. Still serenity eludes us like the butterfly we seek to catch and possess. Once we discover our omnipresent spirituality we understand and experience that serenity is a gift from God that we humbly ask to receive. The butterfly lands and lights on us when we least expect it.

As adults we wrap ourselves in so much illusion and lose sight of what is really important in life. We find it difficult to live life. Despite our intellect, reason, and decades of experience we find ourselves overwhelmed by home, career, kids, school, soccer games, and so on. Yet it is the metaphysical realities of this world that ironically turn our understanding on its head.

If the mundane, everyday challenges that we face as adults send us into a tail-spin, how can a mere child face death with serenity? This amazing story of a cou-rageous young man who grew into an adult while battling leukemia will answer that question. In the prime of his health Chris always saw the joy and the humor in simple situations. Yet, even as that great monster cancer overwhelmed Chris's physical presence he never lost that special ability to cherish each moment.

The genetic origin of this sense of humor would be clear to all who know Chris's parents and relatives. Practical jokes, bathroom humor, stupid blonde jokes, bending if not breaking the rules, thinking outside the box; all of that went a long way to allow Chris and his family to face death and still laugh along their journey to seek a cure for leukemia.

For those who read the story of *Christopher's Journey* as told by his mother life lessons await. Read on, and come to know the wise old soul that lived in Chris's body.

Introduction

It's bittersweet to remember the times before the cancer came into our lives. Chris would often refer to them as "the good old days." He would speak of family vacations when he had the energy to splash in the water and shimmy to the top of palm trees. Back then catching lizards and crawling through cardboard box fortresses were the stuff his days were made of. But at the age of ten his childhood was abruptly snatched away, and all he had were the memories of a lost youth. So, by the tender age of fourteen he had earned the right to use such phrases as "the good old days," phrases normally reserved for the elderly. Chris had spent the last four years of his life living with leukemia.

"Cancer years are like dog years," we'd joke. "You age seven years for every one year." But it was really true in so many ways. We had watched in awe as we raised this amazing man-child who responded to pain and adversity with humor and affection. The cancer gradually robbed him of his energy, and eventually his life, but it could not steal Chris's spirit, his insatiable ability to love; that was the private property of Chris and a higher power. Later, our friend and parish priest, Father John, would refer to Chris as an "old soul." I think he was right.

This is the story of Chris's journey through childhood leukemia, but it is much more than Chris's story. It is the story of our family's struggle, and of countless people who were touched along the way. It is also a survival manual of sorts on how to cope with a life-threatening illness, how to talk about life and death with children, and how to play really good practical jokes in a pediatric hospital.

This book is also an account of the many lessons Chris taught us. He taught us how one can still live with cancer and find love and humor in the most unlikely places. Chris also taught us about death. From him we learned not to fear it, but when the time comes, to embrace it. Our son, lover of animals and adventure, shall always be our guide on the greatest adventure that awaits us all: our journey into the next life. So Christopher's journey becomes our journey.

PART I

CHRIS'S FIRST PROTOCOL: 1997–1998

1

A DANGEROUS DIAGNOSIS

The last of "the good old days" had begun with a family vacation in June of 1997. We had trailered our boat down to our favorite spot in the Florida Keys: an idyllic strip of land in the lower middle Keys, Bahia Honda State Park. Twelve of us had rented two side-by-side cabins, standing tall on stilts looking over the turquoise, fish-filled waters of the Florida Bay. There were the five of us, my husband, Bob, our fourteen-year-old daughter, Erin, ten-year-old Chris, and three-year-old Jarrod. Joining us were my parents, my sister, her husband, and a fun-loving band of cousins. But during the week Chris had grown increasingly lethargic, not his usual scampering, tree-climbing self. While the rest of us skied and snorkeled Chris had been content to sit in the boat, huddled under a towel. When I had found a nurse shark peeking out from a watery crevice beneath the boat I was certain that Chris would plunge in, fearless and full of adventure as always. But he had chosen to stay in the boat. "The water's cold," he'd said.

"C'mon, the water's ninety degrees!" we'd responded. We didn't know that his bone marrow was producing rapidly dividing cancer cells, immature mutated "blasts" instead of normal, healthy cells. These errant cells were choking out his precious red cells, the ones carrying oxygen and warmth throughout his body. Without a proper supply of oxygen, his energy had waned. Finally, just a few days later, he couldn't make it up the steps of our cabin without clutching his chest and gasping for air. It was at that moment, watching him sitting helpless on the stairs, that I had known something was terribly wrong.

We didn't even have a phone in the cabin so I had followed the coral pathway to a campground pay phone and called our family doctor. "We'll be there first thing Monday morning ... Please do every test that you can possibly think of."

That night I had slept poorly, tossing about with strange dreams. We were having tile put in our house while we were away, and I dreamed that they put in the wrong tile. At first it seemed to resemble the pale peach fourteen-inch tile that we had selected, but in the dream I watched the tile slowly start to move and

3

mutate into dark, misshapen shards. Later, I would discover that this dream was a premonition.

I had another premonition on the long ride home the following day. It was slow going, towing our boat along the narrow Florida Route 1, and across the infamous "Alligator Alley," a two-lane highway full of vacationers and summer thunderstorms. I kept thinking of a television series I used to watch. It was about a teenage genius who had graduated from medical school before most adolescents his age had completed high school. In the program the young doctor had stated that his primary motivation for entering the medical field was his own experience as a survivor of childhood leukemia. I just couldn't get that show out of my mind.

On Monday morning, June 30, we had a 10:00-AM appointment with our family practitioner, Doctor Rubin. During the seven-hour drive home from the Keys I had written down Chris's list of symptoms. Now as Chris lay on the examining table I pulled the carefully folded sheet of paper out of my pocket.

Chris's Symptoms:

*Stomach cramps after eating
*Daily headaches
* Tires easily—does not run around and climb trees any more. Does not enjoy bike riding
*Pain in center of chest after exercise
*Complains of legs hurting after climbing stairs
* Looks pale
*Poor appetite

As I shared my list I remembered feeling guilty and negligent for not bringing Chris in sooner. I recalled an incident just before our trip in which Chris, as was his usual custom, was riding his bike beside me while I jogged around the neighborhood. He'd stopped early before we completed our three-mile loop. "I'm tired; I think I'll go home," he'd said. Until I had taken the trouble to jot them down I just hadn't realized how many odd symptoms he had. I felt terrible for taking him on vacation, dismissing his ailments as nothing. Now as the doctor examined him he noted that Chris's spleen and lymph nodes were swollen. "It could be lots of things," he said calmly. "Let's do some blood tests. We'll get back to you in forty-eight hours."

I didn't say anything in front of Chris, but my brain was screaming, "CANCER, CANCER, CANCER!" I just kept thinking about that show about the boy who'd had leukemia. I had an awful feeling, and I never have awful feelings. "Whatever it is," I told Chris, "they'll figure it out and fix it."

"I know, Mom." Chris replied. He trusted us implicitly. That trust was going to have to go a very long way.

We were only home three or four hours when the phone rang and I snatched it up. "This is Dr. Rubin." Immediately my heart started pounding. It wasn't a nurse or a lab technician; it was the doctor himself. Secretaries call you with good news. Doctors call you with bad news.

He spoke calmly, and I'm certain he had to repeat himself to me several times, "It's leukemia."

"Are you absolutely sure?" I gasped.

"I can tell from the lab work," Dr. Rubin said. "A normal white cell count is between four thousand and ten thousand. Chris's is seven hundred thousand. You need to get him up to All Children's Hospital immediately. It's in Saint Petersburg. If the oncology clinic is closed, go to the emergency room. I called them and told them you are coming."

Briefly he explained that leukemia is cancer of the blood. Immature, ill-formed white cells divide uncontrollably and interfere with the growth and function of healthy cells. This takes place in the bone marrow, which is like a factory where all new blood cells are manufactured. When the cancer cells begin circulating throughout the body they often settle in the spleen and lymph nodes. This explained Chris's symptoms. It's odd that I was able to recall his clinical explanation given the fact that I also had to digest the knowledge that Chris's life was seriously in danger. But that's how my brain seems to work in a crisis—it either shuts down completely or it races to grasp and clarify every parcel of information possible. Dr. Rubin also tried to reassure me about the wonderful new treatments available and the improved cure rate, but he was emphatic that we get Chris to the hospital right away. Our local hospital did not have a pediatric oncology unit, so we would need to drive an hour up to St. Petersburg to All Children's Hospital. But first, we had to tell our ten-year-old son he had cancer.

Chris sat on the edge of the sofa in our family room, the summer sun filtering through the sliding glass door behind him. I could see the fingerprints on the glass. Those were the prints of a little boy whose greatest worry had been a lost homework paper or a squabble with his pesky little brother. Now, in an instant, that was changed forever. How I wished my only concern was to wipe away those prints. How I wished I could wipe away this nightmare.

Chris had always been an intuitive child, and he immediately sensed the gravity of the situation.

"Honey, we have to talk to you. You know how you've been feeling really tired lately? Well, the doctor called and told us what's causing it. It's a problem with some bad cells in your blood. They are going to give you some medicine to help you get better."

The conversation remained calm until we came to the "C" word, but it had to be said. I had been a schoolteacher for sixteen years and had learned early on that children deserved to be told the truth. They are much better at spotting lies and cover-ups than we adults give them credit for. And I knew that Chris needed to hear that word first from us, not from a stranger.

Tears welled up in his eyes, and I noticed how skinny and vulnerable he looked. "I have cancer! Am I going to die?"

"No, the doctor said the kind of cancer you have, leukemia, is one of the easiest kinds to cure. You aren't going to die." Bob and I repeated that several times, as much to convince ourselves as to convince Chris. We were adamant that cancer did not equal death. So now we had to prepare to live with it.

We arrived at the medical building across the street from the hospital just before 5:00 PM so we were spared a trip to the emergency room. I'll never forget walking down that long carpeted hallway for the first time. There were prints of tropical fish that seemed out of place in the frigid air-conditioning. The Pediatric Oncology Clinic was the last office at the end, and it seemed like it took forever to find it. We had begun our very long journey into the strange and frightening world of childhood cancer. I had no idea how many hundreds and hundreds of times we would walk down that hallway over the next several years. At some point during the confusion and fear that day, I decided that it would be a good idea to write everything down. And that was the beginning of my journal. The entries would continue for four more years, almost to the day.

June 30, 1997

... At 5:00 Chris was seen by oncologist, Dr. Rossbach, who confirmed the diagnosis of leukemia. Chris was immediately admitted to the intensive care unit. There we met the head oncologist, Dr. Barbosa, the ICU doctor, Chaplin Paul, and other professionals and nurses. Bombarded with information! This is what I learned: ALL is acute lymphoblastic (sometimes referred to as lymphocytic) leukemia. Also learned about chemotherapy ...

My first few entries were devoid of emotion. Sometimes they were mere lists of medications and chemotherapy drugs. They reflected my state of shock and disbelief. It felt as if we were actors in a very bad play. Also tantamount were the sense of helplessness, and the sudden loss of control over our lives. Being an educator, the only way I could gain any sense of power was to learn as much as I could as quickly as I could. It was like cramming for the worst final exam any student ever had, and the penalty for failure was death. Not my death, but my child's death!

That first day in the hospital we also met the nurse educator Tessa. She was a short, stout, no-nonsense type, but she was also compassionate. She was the one who handed us sheet after sheet of consent forms and drug information charts. She was the one who had the time to sit and patiently answer our endless questions. She was my new best friend.

From her we learned that ALL was the most common, and the most curable, form of childhood leukemia. The cure rate was currently between 75 and 80 percent. Bob and I clung to that statistic like a drowning man clings to a raft. We would quote it over and over again during countless phone conversations. "Yes, Chris has leukemia," we told family and friends, "but his kind is highly curable. Most of the kids survive."

We found ourselves in the strange position of not only having to explain Chris's disease, but also having to comfort others who sometimes wept at the other end of the phone.

"Oh God, I heard the news," lamented one well-meaning friend. "How awful! You must be devastated."

"Well, the drug treatments nowadays are quite effective ..." I would find myself launching into a litany of hope, slipping unconsciously into the teacher role, reassuring others. It was mentally exhausting. What I really wanted to do was tear out into the hallway and let out an enormous primal scream. After a while we came to the realization that the world wouldn't stop if we weren't available for phone calls. We had to remind ourselves to focus all of our energy on Chris. Others could wait.

Tessa also explained that Chris would be given combinations of powerful drugs known collectively as chemotherapy. They work simply by attacking the most rapidly dividing cells in the body. Since unusually rapid cell growth is the hallmark of cancer, the chemotherapy homes in on it. I took notes as she spoke. It was my only way of controlling what little there was for me to control: my knowledge.

Unfortunately, chemotherapy attacks some of the body's healthy cells as well. Tessa went on to explain that a lot of chemotherapy patients lose their hair because the hair follicles grow quickly, so they fall prey to the chemo. The mucus lining of the mouth and digestive tract are also susceptible, leading to mouth sores and nausea. Tears welled up in my eyes as she explained the horrible-sounding drugs with endless lists of side effects. I couldn't help but wonder if the cure wasn't worse than the disease.

We also had to face the sobering fact that Chris's treatment protocol was LONG. It involved seven months of hospital admissions followed by two years of maintenance outpatient treatment. This was to become our new life.

And so began the first of many conversations we would have with Chris, steeling our resolve to digest this harsh new reality and interpret it back to him without scaring him to death, without letting him see that we were scared to death.

"Mom, am I going to die?" he had asked again, after being placed in the intensive care unit, and having several IVs inserted into his arms and into one of his legs.

"No, Chris, you aren't going to die. They are going to give you a lot of medicine to kill the cancer in your blood. Some of the medicine might make you sick, but you aren't going to die." Now I just had to convince myself that that was true.

I wrote down every scrap of information that I could.

July 1, 1997

Chris's white count is so high that he had to undergo a process called leukopheresis to filter out the cancer cells. I can see the machine spinning, and the blood moving out of his body in a tube, into a bag, then the filtered blood going back into his body. I can actually see the white cells in the bag!

Today, I learned more from Dr. Rossbach about the drugs Chris will be given: prednisone (by mouth—PO), vincristine (IV), L-asparaginase (intermuscular shot—IM), and daunomycin (IV). Even the names sound nauseous.

As the drugs were introduced into Chris's system, the side effects began. His blood pressure went up, and he experienced headaches and nausea. But Chris remained his humorous self. "Tell them to give me teenager blood so I can be cool."

He lay in the bed playing with an action figure, making the appropriate little boy zooming noises. "Batman has a porta-potty in his flight suit, know why?"

"Why?" asked the nurse.

"Because he gets nervous." Chris stretched his arm, holding the figure high above his head, and blew raspberries to simulate that favorite boyhood preoccupation, bowel movements. Comments like this would become Chris's trademark. No one ever knew what he was going to say. I was so proud of him.

On the third day I learned about "tumorlysis syndrome." When cancer cells are rapidly broken down they release chemicals into the blood stream, and they can cause dangerous chemical imbalances in the body. It was as if there was a Star Wars battle going on inside of Chris's body. And all I could do was sit by helplessly and watch.

July 2, 1997

Bad Morning! Chris's potassium level became dangerously high. He tried for thirty or forty minutes to swallow the medicine that would lower it, and was not able to. "This stuff is nasty!" he gagged.

Dr. Rossbach told Chris point blank if he didn't take the medicine he could die.

"Well, how much do I have to drink?" Chris asked.

Dr. Rossbach held up a vial and said, "Two of these."

"No way."

"If you don't drink it we are going to have to put a tube down your nose and give it to you that way. So why don't you drink it?"

At this point, both Chris and I knew that just wasn't going to happen.

"I'll take the tube," Chris announced.

Then the doctor asked us to leave the room. Bob left, but I refused. There was a moment when they all stood there in silence, waiting for me to acquiesce, but there was no way I was going to leave my son's side.

"Chris, do you want me to stay?"

"Yes, Mom."

So I stayed by my son's side.

Chris didn't tolerate the tube well. He threw up several times and said, "I love you, Mom" between pukes. I held him and told him it was going to be OK, the medicine would make him better. I sang him "The Moonpuppy Song." It was very hard for both of us, but I was glad that I stayed by his side.

The "Moonpuppy Song" was a song I'd made up about our black Labrador retriever, Moonshine. I had swiped the tune from the Cat Stevens song, "Moonshadow," and rewritten it for our dog. It had been part of our bedtime ritual when Chris was younger. It seemed to calm him down, and as I sang I pretended that all of the machines and medical personnel had vanished, and there was just a mom singing her little boy to sleep.

My refusal to leave during the insertion of the feeding tube became the first of many times that I would assert myself. Eventually the staff would grow to trust and respect us, allowing us to be with Chris for different procedures and make decisions concerning his treatment. In the beginning the hospital setting was very intimidating with its high-tech equipment and sometimes brusque and authoritative doctors. But we were the experts when it came to our son. We knew when he was in pain, and when he was frightened. We knew the songs and jokes that could calm him down and help him to cope. We learned quickly which pain medications worked, and which ones didn't. Overnight we had become his advocates in a strange new world.

On the fourth day Chris's white count and blood chemistry were back in the normal range so he made it out of ICU and up onto the oncology floor, 2 Southwest, our new home away from home. With its brightly painted doorways and colorful stencils on the walls it was a cheerful contrast to the intensive care unit. We had the opportunity to speak more with the head oncologist, Dr. Barbosa. He was a husky man who smiled more readily than the smaller, more intense Dr. Rossbach. Both spoke with foreign accents, Dr. Barbosa's from Bolivia, and Dr. Rossbach's German. This, combined with all the unfamiliar medical jargon, made me feel overwhelmed at times.

The nurses were friendly and warm. One of them informed Chris that he would be granted a wish from an organization such as The Make A Wish Foundation. Chris was in good spirits and asked questions about potential wishes. Limo rides with movie stars and trips to snowy places were his top choices. For the first time since we had learned of his illness Chris showed signs of his old sparkle and enthusiasm.

"Mom, do you think I should wish to meet Kevin Bacon or go snowboarding?"

"Definitely snowboarding," I replied, "That would last longer, and I'd get to go skiing." I had grown up in the northeast and had developed a passion for snow skiing. So once a year I bundled up whomever wanted to accompany me and we headed north to visit family and play in the snow. So, despite having lived in Florida all of his young life, Chris had gone skiing or boarding since he was potty trained.

"I know, I'll go snowboarding with Kevin Bacon!" Chris exclaimed. "We'll chill out together, then he'll invite me to be in a movie with him."

But the jocularity was short lived. Chris had to be prepared for surgery. He would have a catheter called a "mediport" inserted into his chest. This would allow the staff to administer his many intravenous drugs without puncturing his veins. In the long run it would save Chris the pain of multiple sticks and collapsed veins. So we went from daydreaming about wishes back to the present reality. That's the way it would be on the oncology floor, quick snatches of fun sandwiched into the painful routines. Each day brought more information overload.

July 4, 1997

Chris slept well last night, but threw up right after they gave him his pills. The nurse put on rubber gloves and peered into the bucket to see if the pills stayed down. Yuck.… Tessa showed Bob and me how to read the important numbers on Chris's lab report and how to calculate the ANC, Absolute Neutrophil Count. This is vitally important because it is a measure of how strong his immune system is. Neutrophils are the white blood cells that fight infection … His treatment protocol is in three stages: Induction, which is one month; Consolidation, also known as Intensification, which lasts five or six months; and finally Maintenance, which is two years …

When Chris wasn't looking tears of reality burned my checks, and I jotted down my questions. If one nurse didn't know an answer I found one who did. I hovered in the hallway, waiting for the doctor to make his rounds and arrive at Chris's door. I started to learn the tricks for surviving in the hospital, like making sure Chris had medications listed in his orders for both pain and nausea. Otherwise, poor Chris would have to wait an agonizingly long time while a nurse paged the on-call doctor. I also wrote down his doses and how often he was to receive them. This was especially key for pain management. For example, if Chris was allowed a dose of morphine every six hours, I made sure that this was taken care of before shift change. Shift change involved the departing staff giving "report" to the incoming crew. If the floor was full, this process could take well over an hour. When you are in pain an hour may as well be a month.

Fortunately, I was blessed with a gregarious, outgoing personality. So although I could be a pest, I was a friendly pest. I asked the nurses about their families and swapped jokes with them. Chris had inherited my knack for humor and soon he had everyone charmed. He could impersonate the deep alien voice of the movie character "ET," as well as assorted cartoon characters. When a nurse would come in to hang a bag of chemo on his infusion pump, "ET" would moan, "AHHHH Chem-ooo-therrrr-apy!"

We learned very quickly to live in the moment. An hour of fun playing pool in the playroom was often followed by several hours of misery. The side effects of the chemotherapy ebbed and flowed throughout the day. And some days were definitely better than others.

July 6, 1997

This morning Chris had a lot of nausea and headaches ... The codeine worked for a while on the headaches, but Chris ended up throwing up all of his Spaghetti-o's, so we put him back on morphine and let him sleep ... Later was better. This time the Spaghetti-o's stayed down. We watched a movie and Chris played Nintendo. "Do you know what my Gerbil, Max, is doing right now, Mom?" Chris asked me.

"No, what?" I pictured Chris's empty room at home, wishing he could be there.

"He's in his cage making me a teeny little get well card with a sunflower seed in it." Chris fidgeted with his fingers as if he were wrapping a gift and made tiny little rodent-like squeaks.

I laughed and laughed.

Overall—Bad day, Good evening.

Another harsh reality that hit us that first admission was the issue of finances. Suddenly we were faced with having to spend large amounts of time at the hospital, which meant lost work time and lost wages. Bob had some flexibility as he is a self-employed subcontractor, but I am a schoolteacher with a rigid schedule. What would I do in the fall when school would resume? We depended on both our incomes. I couldn't quit my job to care for Chris even if we could manage without my salary because we depended on the school board for the medical coverage. But how could I work all day with other peoples' healthy children knowing my son needed me? And how much would we have to spend on all of his hospitalizations and prescriptions? We had insurance, but we knew the co-pays wouldn't take long to mount.

The combined stress of Chris's precarious health and our uncertain financial future was enormous. I had to make the very conscious decision not to dwell on the money worries and simply focus on being there for Chris. This was not easy to do, and the sleepless nights took their toll.

But at the same time it seemed a network of angels was forming around us, and help was on the way. That first week began our long relationship with The Ronald McDonald House, an organization that I can't praise enough. The Ronald McDonald House Charities operate over two hundred houses around the world. They are located near hospitals and provide a place to stay for families of sick children. Volunteers cook homemade meals and offer a sympathetic ear to your troubles. The many services include free laundry, long-distance calling cards, tickets to local sports events and museums, and direct phone access from your room to your child's hospital room. This meant I could flop into a comfortable bed right across the street and the nurses could summon me at a moment's notice. We were extremely fortunate that All Children's Hospital had two Ronald McDonald houses to service it. It didn't take long for us to become well acquainted with the staff and volunteers there.

I'll never forget the first time I walked down the steps to the laundry room at the RMH. There on the floor was that unmistakable tile from the dream that I'd had back in the Keys, right before Chris was diagnosed! Dark earth tones cut into irregular pie-shaped pieces. I had never seen tile like it anywhere else except in that bizarre dream, and I had completely forgotten about it until I stood there frozen in the doorway.

Back at home meals began to appear on our doorstep. Offers to help with Erin and Jarrod came pouring in. As the word spread about Chris's illness we became the recipients of many acts of kindness. One day Dorothy Aldor, the owner of the preschool Jarrod attended, called. "I just want you and Bob to know how much we are all praying for Chris (both Erin and Chris had attended the same school). And we won't take any more money for Jarrod's daycare. He's free from now on."

This was the beginning of what was to become a long spiritual journey for me. I had always been a practicing Catholic, but at times the rituals of the mass had felt mechanical, like lines memorized for a play. As a child I had been taught that it was a sin to miss mass on Sunday, but as an adult I had certainly committed that sin when it just wasn't convenient to go. "That's why I'm a practicing Catholic," I'd joke, "I'll just have to keep practicing until I get it right." Now I was facing the biggest crisis of my life, every parent's worst nightmare—a child with a life-threatening illness. If ever there was an opportunity to get furious with God, this was it. But I just couldn't stay mad at God, because every time I tried to someone would interrupt with an act of kindness.

Lynda, the hospital social worker, was another angel. She gave us information on various cancer organizations that could help with tardy bills and reimbursements for prescriptions and mileage. It made us feel as if there were a safety net to catch us if we fell. It was also a humbling experience, for we had never needed to ask anyone for help before. We lived a comfortable, middle-class lifestyle, and were always the type who gave at the office, not the ones who accepted assistance.

But cancer is a great equalizer. It knows no socio-economic boundaries, and we soon discovered we had lots of company in this new uncertain existence.

A hospital oncology unit is a community unto itself. Because the treatment protocols for cancer can be very lengthy, the same children keep coming back, so the names and faces become familiar. 2 Southwest is a hematology oncology floor that services a variety of cancers, as well as blood disorders such as hemophilia and sickle cell anemia. I became attached to the children there just as I would my own students in the classroom.

Chris's very first roommate on 2 Southwest was a boy named Kevin. He was one year into his treatment for t-cell leukemia. Chris had a more common form called pre-B-cell leukemia. The letters denoted the particular cell subgroup that had gone haywire. Based upon research and clinical studies, each specific type of leukemia has its own recommended treatment cocktail of drugs. But when I looked at the two little boys in the room together playing video games and watching TV, I knew they weren't thinking about all of that. They were just being boys, having to push an IV pole everywhere they went, having to pee into a cc-calibrated urinal, but still little boys. Like Chris, Kevin had a sprinkling of freckles across his nose, but he was completely bald. I thought he was adorable and wanted to kiss him on top of the head like you would a newborn. Chris had been told that he would lose his hair also, so I guess it was good for him to see Kevin playing and not being self-conscious about his appearance.

Kevin's mom, Jane, was very helpful. She told me what to expect when we took Chris home between treatments. She explained that his counts would drop then slowly recover. When they were down he would be very immuniosupressed and would need to be protected from germs. She offered practical suggestions like renting videos and attending uncrowded matinees. She had organized all of Kevin's drug information handouts into a notebook for easy reference, so I decided to do the same with my materials.

Brett McDonald was another young leukemia patient the same age as Chris. Our first few days there, his mother, Tara, approached me and asked if I remembered her. Chris and Brett had gone to preschool together, the same school that Jarrod now attended. What an odd reunion. Tara was also kind and helpful. It was an enormous relief for me to see other families managing to function under such trying circumstances. We all shared an instant camaraderie, like soldiers trapped in the trenches with shells exploding all around us.

Finally, after nine days of intense chemotherapy Chris was ready to go home for a little while. We had a daunting list of daily medications that had to be administered, and I felt like a new mother taking her baby home for the first time. Would I know how to take care of him properly?

July 8, 1997

Tessa spent a lot of time with me today explaining Chris's drug schedule, so now I feel like I understand it ... I met a female oncologist, Dr. Grana. She speaks with a Puerto Rican accent which is sometimes hard to understand, but she seemed very patient about answering questions ... I am nervous about Chris's problems taking pills. Chris was unsuccessful taking his morning prednisone. It came right back up. Will try crushing it in applesauce. *Note* Buy applesauce when we get home. What I learned today: Important things on the lab report are WBC (white blood count), hemoglobin (red cells), platelets (cells that clot to control bleeding), and blasts (leukemia cells).

2

THE QUEST FOR REMISSION

The first thirty days of Chris's treatment, the induction period, were key because that was when the doctors expected Chris to gain remission. That meant having no detectable leukemia in his blood. So on July 29 when they did a bone marrow aspiration (this involved inserting a needle into the bony portion of his back to extract a sample of bone marrow) we were thrilled to learn that he was, indeed, in remission. His treatment, however, was far from over.

This began thirty weeks of life in and out of the hospital. It usually went something like this: five or six days of inpatient chemotherapy followed by twelve to fourteen days at home, then back in for more chemotherapy. Because of his initially very high white count, Chris was classified as a high-risk patient and given the largest allowable therapeutic doses. This meant lots of side effects. They included body aches, fatigue, mouth sores, nausea, and sometimes fevers. If Chris's temperature reached 38.3 degrees C (101degrees F), that meant he had to be admitted to the hospital for intravenous antibiotics. Fevers in an immuniosuppressed patient can be an indicator of serious infection. As a result, we sometimes had additional, unscheduled hospital stays.

The quality of the time at home depended upon where Chris was in his treatment cycle. Generally, it took seven to ten days for the chemotherapy to knock his counts down. Then he would gradually recover, and just as Chris began to feel like his old self again, it was time to return to the hospital for more treatment. We kept track of his immune status with twice weekly labwork. This told us how "down" his immune system was, and whether or not he needed to be isolated. After a while we were able to count the days after a hospitalization and predict fairly accurately how immuniosuppressed he would be at different times. Needless to say, our lives had completely changed, and were now ruled by Chris's treatments. Activities such as birthday parties, ball games, and trips to the movies were possible only a few days a month.

The other unwilling victims of this situation were Chris's teenage sister, Erin, and his three-year-old brother, Jarrod. Until now we had enjoyed a traditional family lifestyle with both parents and three children sitting down together for dinner each night. Erin was a ballet dancer, and Chris, a soccer player. Then suddenly, none of that seemed important anymore. Everything became focused on keeping Chris alive, getting his pills down, taking his temperature, relieving the pain of his side effects, and shuttling back and forth to the hospital.

"If Chris had done that you wouldn't yell at him!" became Erin's war chant. Or "How come I have to do his chores now?" We did the best that we could to explain that it was difficult to empty trash while one is throwing up, but a fourteen-year-old's world is an egocentric one, and communication is precarious.

For Jarrod it was, "Mommy, how come you have to go to the hospital again? When will you be home?"

So Bob and I just kept telling them that we loved them, and we wished things were different, but that was the way it was and we had to deal with it. Because of our situation we all had "extra chores." Chris's were the toughest of all. We had to stick together as a family. Easier said than done.

During one such family squabble I remember watching Erin flounce past me down the hall slamming the door to her bedroom. It was tempting to chase after her and yell back, and sometimes that's exactly what I did, but not that time. We had to make room for a couple of new family members, I told myself: anger and fear.

My nighttime prayers had changed from the usual Hail Mary's and God bless so and so's to "Lord, give me the courage to help my family get through this. Please watch over Chris and let him get into remission. Give me the strength to get out of bed tomorrow and make it through the day."

The next hospital admission brought an answer to our prayers for remission.

July 29, 1997

Induction Success! Chris's bone marrow was negative for leukemia. Today we signed the consent forms for Chris to be in a clinical study. He was admitted to the hospital for the beginning of the consolidation therapy ... He's in the same room as last time, and has the same roommate, Kevin. Chris felt well, and the boys were able to play together ... While we were excited about Chris's remission Chris was equally thrilled with the fact that an empty syringe makes an outstanding water pistol!

July 30, 1997

... Chris had a spinal tap, and they put chemo into his spinal fluid to prevent the leukemia from spreading to the brain. They gave him a drug called fentanyl so he doesn't feel anything. It made him high as a kite and he told Dr. Barbosa that he was the best doctor in the whole world. The nurse in the room also happened to be the best nurse in the entire world. And I knew where I ranked on the "mom" scale as well ...

... Went to a parent support group today—very emotional, but worthwhile. I met a lot of parents on the floor. There's Dina, Tanya's mom. Tanya is a little girl with leukemia who just had a bone marrow transplant. The transplant process is extremely difficult and I hope Chris never has to go through that. Also met some parents of teens with cancer. Several were single parents. Some had no insurance and had been wiped out financially. Amazing how a person can feel lucky even in a place like this ...

... We got the results of our blood tests (HLA typing) today. Should Chris end up needing a bone marrow transplant, no one in our family matches ...

Chris's next hospital visit dragged on for two weeks, and that's when we really learned to *carpe diem,* seize the day. He developed painful side effects and high fevers from the chemo drug, methotrexate (MTX for short). His left wrist also became inflamed and they were concerned about infection. He had to be given antibiotics, and was put on a morphine drip. Despite this, he had periods of time when he could play and have fun.

August 2, 1997

Chris had great fun playing cards with Jarrod. Because his hospital bed was higher than Jarrod's chair, Chris had full view of Jarrod's hand, and Jarrod, of course, was clueless. Chris amazed and astounded Jarrod with his "ability" to detect what was in Jarrod's hand.

"Chris, how did you know I had two jacks?" Jarrod gazed at his brother in awe.

"Must be the cancer," Chris teased, "It gives me magic powers."

"Wow, I hope I get "kemia" (Jarrod's name for leukemia) too."

At that point I couldn't stand the thought of Jarrod wishing for cancer so I blew the whistle on Chris.

It didn't take us long to figure out which staff members were ripe for "picking." Our favorite target was Nurse Nancy. Chris and I both decided that when she was born the doctors had used a big rubber stamp upon her buttocks that read, "Pick on Me." That, plus the fact that she teased us back relentlessly, led to a very entertaining love-hate relationship. An additional bonus was the fact that Nancy was blonde. Our logical conclusion was that she was the intended recipient of any blonde joke ever written.

August 8, 1997

Finally, no fever all night. Chris actually took a shower and ate for the first time in over a week. He hid a syringe loaded with water under the sheets and squirted Nancy when she came in. "Ditmars' mother," she said to me (she never used my given name), "Can't you control your pesky child?"

"I thought he had lots of control on that shot. He got you in the face without getting your hair wet. That takes lots of control!" I countered.

"Yeah, and you don't smell so bad when you're wet, Smelly Melly," Chris added. (Nancy's last name was "Melly.")

"Well, I'm going to go take care of some of my nice patients! But don't worry, I don't get mad, I get even ..."

Another favorite hospital pastime was Chris's wish list. Once he found out that he was eligible for a wish Chris enjoyed adding to and revising it daily. The most popular items included: A trip to Hollywood with the Hanson Brothers (a popular rock band at the time), singing in a music video, appearing in a James Bond movie, riding in a limo then appearing in a James Bond movie, going snowboarding with Kevin Bacon, Chris's favorite actor, going on a shopping spree at the mall, riding in a limo to a shopping spree at the mall, and going on a cruise on the brand-new Disney ship.

Of course I had heard of Make A Wish and similar organizations before, but hadn't ever given them much thought. Like many people, I'd had the mistaken impression that the wishes were offered only to terminally ill patients. I had seen news stories about children going to Disney World or meeting a famous sports figure, and I had said to myself, "Isn't that nice that they get to do that before they die." Never had I imagined that my child would qualify to receive a wish. The criteria is that the child have a "life-threatening illness." So it was with bittersweet reflection that I pondered Chris's opportunity for a wish. It was wonderful that it was being offered; yet it was sobering to realize that the reason behind it was that he might not survive his illness.

After much discussion and after speaking to a representative from a local wish organization, The Suncoast Children's Dream Foundation, Chris chose the Disney Cruise. They had warned him that celebrity wishes were unpredictable, and not all celebrities are generous with their time. Sometimes all they do is see you for a few minutes and sign an autograph. A family trip together would last several days, and would be a cherished memory for the whole family. So being the unselfish person that he was, Chris wasn't just thinking of himself when he chose the cruise.

After that decision was made Chris pored over the brochure and the map of the ship. Before long he knew the layout and could show us where all of the restaurants, swimming pools, and game rooms were. "When we get on board, I'll show you around," he said proudly. This wish was to be the first of the Cancer Perks (CPs, I would later call them), the neat stuff donated to young cancer patients. With all the suffering they endured, Lord knows they needed a few perks.

August 8, 1997 cont'd

... Chris's roommate is an adorable little Hispanic baby named Jasmine. (Kevin went home a few days ago.) She has ALL also and is only nine months old. Her mom is Diana—very sweet, very calm. Dad, Tony, is like a big kid. He looks like he's only nineteen or twenty. Chris enjoys his company ...

... The St. Jude telethon was on TV, and Chris and I watched some stories of other children with leukemia. I think he was struck by the fact that he would be returning to the hospital again and again. It's going to be a long struggle.

Sitting in a hospital room watching a telethon featuring other families facing the same ordeal that we were was both comforting and disquieting at the same time. I felt as if we were now living in a parallel universe. We drove on the same streets and breathed the same air as the rest of the world, but we lived a whole different reality. I envisioned a giant map of the United States dotted with hospitals, and inside them other children like Chris. The program portrayed its young patients as heroes, and rightly so. Chris was now among those ranks, isolated behind the hospital walls fighting the enemy inside him, joined in spirit with all of those other patients. It seemed like we were all waiting for the telethon viewers to donate enough money to find a cure, hoping that it would come in time to save our children.

August 9, 1997

Chris continues to be without fever. Dr. Barbosa is still a little concerned about his wrist. He doesn't want any infection to get into the bone ... so they will continue with antibiotics ... Now that Chris is eating a little bit they can take him off of the Hyper-alimentation (IV food) ... The doctors and nurses are all telling Chris that he needs to get out of bed and walk around. Nurse Gerri fed Chris some Pediacare milk shake with a syringe and we got him to go to the playroom. We played Scrabble (Chris could always manage to find the right letters to spell "fart" and "poop") video games, and then went to the rooftop playground for a while—much improved activity level.

I spoke with Dina McKenzie again. She's hoping to take Tanya home a week from Monday. Because she's a transplant patient they have been here for weeks ... Also talked and joked about RMH (The Ronald McDonald House) chores with Jasmine's mom, Diana.

It didn't take long for me to become attached to the people I met at the hospital and The Ronald McDonald House. Sharing the common bond of having a child with cancer meant that we already knew each other's deepest fears and hopes. We could sit and talk endlessly about our children's treatment protocols, their chances for survival, how we coped with the needs of our other children, and just about any topic under the sun. There wasn't any aspect of our lives that hadn't been affected; therefore everything we shared had a familiar ring to it. We all had lives that had suddenly changed one day when we learned that our children had cancer. It was like we all had our own little Norman Rockwell paintings that someone had washed over in shades of gray. Most importantly, we were great listeners for each other.

Another great support for me was the staff and volunteers at The Ronald McDonald House. Bob and I kept a room there whenever Chris was hospitalized so that one of us could be available for Chris twenty-four hours a day. Some of the parents preferred to sleep in their child's hospital room, but neither of us was ever able to sleep in the pullout chairs next to the frequent interruptions of a beeping IV pump and the glare of fluorescent lights from the hallway. I felt that I could be a better support to Chris if I was rested myself. Of course, there were nights when he had high fevers or he was in a lot of pain, so then I would stay in the room and only leave to catch a few hours of sleep after he was stabilized.

Some of my favorite people at RMH included the day managers Judy and Carla, the director of volunteers, Sally Jo, and the general manager, Donna, who lived next door and oversaw operations of both St. Petersburg Houses. Judy was big and huggable and reminded me of the actress Delta Burke. She even had a similar southern accent. Blonde, athletic-looking Carla was always hustling about, cleaning and organizing as her keys rattled on her belt loop. After Carla found out that Chris loved Spaghettio's and clam chowder, she would frequently unlock the storage room (known as "the dungeon") beneath the kitchen and let me rummage through the canned goods looking for Chris's favorites.

The west house where we stayed was originally a lovely private residence with a Florida style front porch, a barrel tile roof, and roomy upstairs bedrooms. In 1980 when it became a Ronald McDonald House it was renovated and added onto. But the original part of the house that included "the dungeon" was more than one hundred years old, and Carla had lots of interesting tales about strange noises and objects that moved by themselves. "Not ghosts," she would explain, "Just playful, friendly spirits." I had my own theory, that they were angels with a sense of humor. With a caring staff and volunteers that either brought food or cooked dinner several nights a week, the place was filled with love. So I surmised that it had to be angels. Anyway, I never saw any objects move, but I definitely felt a sense of peace whenever I stayed there, and I could almost always sleep.

Finally, on August 10 Chris got to go home for a few days, but he was due back on the thirteenth. The unexpected length of his previous stay meant precious little time at home. In order for Chris to stay in remission, the doctors stressed that it was very important that Chris follow the treatment schedule.

3

LIFE IN TREATMENT

August 13, 1997

Chris is back for a planned hospitalization. The new drugs he's getting this time are high dose ARA-C, L-asparaginase, and GCSF. The first two are chemotherapy drugs and the GCSF (Granulocyte Colony Stimulating Factor, also known as neupogen) is a drug that stimulates the growth of good white cells, the ones that fight infection. The HDARA-C is expected to knock his counts way down so he'll need the neupogen to recover ... Visited Diana and Jasmine. I brought Diana a doughnut and I made sure that Nurse Nancy, aka "Smelly Melly," saw my pig earrings, which I told her, reminded me of her ...

... At RMH I met a man named Keith. His son, Keith Jr., is an eighteen-year-old football player who was getting ready to go to college on an athletic scholarship. He fell asleep at the wheel and now he's paralyzed from the neck down! Keith Sr.'s wife, Anna, is also a teacher. They have three other young children at home ...

I thought a lot about that young man who in one instant went from being a promising athlete to a quadriplegic. In comparison I felt fortunate since Chris had been given an excellent (75–80 percent) chance of surviving and eventually leading a normal life. But who's to say which is better: A good chance of survival with a small chance of dying or certain survival with a greatly diminished quality of life? I had already learned one important thing—the quality of life in the hospital depended a lot on one's attitude.

When Chris felt well enough to walk around and interact he was quite the character. Ever since his first hospital admission, when Chaplin Peter had demonstrated how to use an empty syringe as a water pistol, Chris was fond of hiding a loaded syringe in his pocket and wandering up to the nurses' station and firing at his unsuspecting victims. After a while they got smart and would duck when they saw him coming. Except Nurse Nancy, of course. She would load her pockets with the big guns, twenty-cc syringes. She loved a good battle.

Nancy also loved to tease me about my unusual earrings. Since the age of fourteen I had been collecting earrings. My motto has always been "Nothing is too tacky." Since then my collection has grown to over four hundred pairs, and much to the delight of my fourth-grade students I usually had something to wear almost every day to match whatever we were studying. For the rain forest there were parrots, monkeys, leopards, elephants, snakes, and so on. I had globe earrings for geography, pencil earrings for writing, ruler earrings for math, and probably seven or eight different kinds of apple earrings for being a teacher. People always gave me unusual earrings as gifts and sometimes if I couldn't find a pair to match a particular theme, I'd been known to make my own. When we were studying the planets I swiped some of Chris's Star Wars Lego figures and made earrings out of them. So it didn't take long for Nancy to notice my silly earwear.

"Ditmars' mother," she'd say, "What have you got on today? You are so weird."

At this point Chris would usually defend my honor by either squirting Nancy or utilizing our other favorite counterattack measure, a blonde joke. "Smelly Melly, how does a blonde kill a fish? She drowns it!" Chris had quite a few memorized, and each one was worse than the next. The fact that they were bad didn't matter.

"Remember, Chris," I'd say, "If you can't make them laugh, make them groan."

August 14, 1997

Today Tessa trained Bobby and me how to give Chris his neupogen shots. It's a subcutaneous (under the skin) injection. We will have to give them to him at home until his counts recover from the chemo. Chris asked to be included in the training also. We all practiced on an orange, then Bobby and I each gave Tessa a shot. (She just used saline.) She turned down Chris's offer to give her a shot. Our first time doing it at home will be on Saturday.

... Later on I saw Tessa in the hall and I told her that the orange had gone into cardiac arrest and was now in the ICU.

I didn't record the exact day in my journal, but it was that summer that Chris lost his hair for the first time. For weeks he had been interacting with plenty of bald-headed children up at the hospital, and he had been told that hair loss was a strong likelihood, but it was still a traumatic experience for him. I remember we were coming home from an outpatient clinic visit, Chris was in the front passenger seat, and Jarrod was in his car seat in the back. Chris was brushing his fingers through his hair watching the strands fly through the air and onto his lap. He was shedding like a dog. "No!" he'd said, tears in his eyes, his teeth clenched in anger. "I'm not going to lose my hair! I'm not!" But he couldn't help impulsively brushing more and more of it off of his head. He couldn't will it to stay there.

A friend of mine whose daughter had survived Hodgkin's disease had suggested that we shave him at the first sign of hair loss. Some of the other parents at the hospital had recommended that as well. "Sometimes it takes days or even weeks for it all to fall out, and it gets everywhere, especially on the pillowcase." they'd said.

I had tried to suggest this to Chris, but he had adamantly refused. "I'M NOT GOING TO LOSE MY HAIR!" Now here he was, trying to bully his hair into submission. I kept my eyes on the road, blinking back my own tears. It was so unfair. Chris had to suffer through all of that nasty chemotherapy, and now he had to look different too.

"You know, Chris, lots of guys shave their heads anyway. It's in style now."

"I don't care."

"Well, I think you'll look good. It'll make you look older, like a teenager."

"No, it won't. I'll just look like a bald freak."

"Well, that's not what I'll see when I look at you. I'll see your handsome face, and I'll know how brave you are. You should be proud of yourself. Your baldness will be a sign of your courage."

Chris wasn't buying it.

But finally, after two or three days of shedding, Chris agreed to a shave. Bobby offered to shave his head as well, but Chris asked him not to. "No, Dad, we might as well only have one person in the family who's butt-ugly. But, why don't you wait until Erin's asleep and shave her head?" There was just the tiniest trace of a smile on his lips.

All I could say was, "I love you."

During Chris's first inpatient protocol, which lasted from June of 1997 until February of 1998, his hospital admissions alternated between two different drug schedules. He either received high dose ARA-C (HDARA-C) or high dose methotrexate(HDMTX) along with other less potent drugs. The HDARA-C and the HDMTX were very powerful chemotherapy drugs that were given intravenously. Chris received so much methotrexate that it took twenty-four hours to infuse it. When handling the chemo bags the nurses were required to wear gowns and gloves. As one nurse put it, "You don't want to spill any of this stuff on your skin. It's nasty!" And that was the poison that was going into my son's body.

Each type had its characteristic side effects. The ARA-C was known to cause very low counts and high fevers. The MTX caused a condition known as mucositis. Mucositis is when the chemo breaks down the mucusal lining of the mouth and digestive tract. The result is sores that can cover the inside of the mouth and continue all the way down into the colon. This can make both eating and going to the bathroom very painful. The typical treatment is placing the patient on a morphine drip and feeding them soft foods or the hyperalimentation (hyper-al for short).

Not everyone reacted the same to the drugs. Kevin's mom said that the ARA-C was the worst for him. But in Chris's case the MTX was the hardest. He almost always got mucositis. It would break my heart to see him trying to eat with a mouth full of sores. Everyone knows how annoying one canker sore is. Imagine having dozens!

While recording our own trauma in my journal, I sometimes noted significant world events as well.

September 5, 1997

Chris is getting his twenty-four-hour HDMTX. He had a spinal tap today. They do that for two reasons: to put chemo in the spinal fluid which prevents leukemia from getting into the brain, and also to check the fluid to see if it's clear of cancer cells. His results were good—no leukemia in the spinal fluid!

Later on he got nauseous and was given some medication for that. He's also getting another chemo drug called 6 MP ...

Mother Teresa died today. I think saints and cancer patients have a lot in common—suffering. They both deserve a special place in Heaven. The difference between a saint and a cancer patient is that the saint chooses the suffering, and with cancer patients the suffering chooses the patient. Regardless, in the end, they both get to pass "GO" and collect two hundred bucks. God, Chris, I love you so much. How I wish I could take on your suffering for you.

September 6, 1997

Chris slept well last night, but then he threw up this morning and had diarrhea. He did manage to take a shower. Afterward he felt well enough to sit up in his chair.

... At 12:30 Chris got very sick and threw up several times, but then he felt better afterward. He felt well enough to tease his nurse, Adam, and call him "Spike" because of his very short haircut. "Spike" keeps it that way to look more like his patients.

They draw labs once a day to see if the MTX has passed through his system enough for him to go home. It has to be .18, and it was 19.0 last nigh! They'll draw a level this evening between 5:00 PM and 6:00 PM, but it probably won't be down by then.

Today I spoke with Ellaina, Edward's mom. I have talked to her several times before during parent support meetings over the summer. Edward is a teenager who has an unusual type of cancer in his leg and stomach. He has not responded to his chemotherapy. He was scheduled for a bone marrow transplant, but they cancelled it. He has a grim prognosis and is going home to hospice care. Basically, they have told her that they can do no more for him ...

... Until now I never thought much about the fact that being here so much would expose us to the suffering of other families and their children. We meet these other families and immediately share a bond with them since they are going through something similar. Then when their children don't do well, I cry with them. I get scared and wonder if we're next. Brett McDonald (Chris's buddy from preschool) is another one who is not doing well.

We watched Princess Diana's funeral this morning. I can't believe she's gone ... At 8:00 PM we got the results of Chris's MTX level, 1.27, still too high to go home. We have to wait at least another twenty-four hours. Chris cried. He really wanted to go home ...

Being in the hospital so much I had to learn to deal with this "double suffering," Chris's and the suffering of other children around us. I had always been the type who formed attachments easily. As a teacher I had looked forward to each new school year with its fresh batch of students that I would eventually fall in love with. Now it was the Edwards and Kevins and Jasmines that I was rooting for. At stake wasn't how well they learned the three Rs, but whether or not they would survive. I wondered how the nurses coped with it when things weren't going well.

It was during this early September admission that Chris met Johnny Ruzinski, aka "Jo Jo." Jo Jo was the same age as Chris and they became instant friends. They shared a passion for video games and Jo Jo was one of the few patients who could give Chris some good competition. Jo Jo was a Ewing's Sarcoma patient.

Jo Jo helped Chris forget his depression over not being able to go home for a few days. They blasted away with their game controllers while his mom, Anna, and I chatted. They were from Plantation, which is on the east coast of Florida. They lived over three hours away from the hospital. We compared notes and found that the boys shared some common dates in their upcoming hospitalizations, so we were grateful that they would be able to keep each other company.

Bobby and I had become masters at juggling dates and working as a team so that one of us covered the home front while the other one was with Chris. As the summer ended we had to figure out what to do about my employment situation. For years our family had depended on my school board health benefits. Without them we would have been broke after Chris's first hospital admission. Indeed, I had met families who, not having insurance, had to sell their property, go on public assistance, or swallow their pride and accept charity. Despite this, as a mother, I was no longer willing to work full time. I felt that to do so would be abandoning Chris when he needed me the most. In the end we worked out a compromise.

I had the great fortune to work for a boss who was both compassionate and creative. After exploring such options as job-sharing I had run into a dead end. The union contract in the county where I taught was inflexible on such matters. I didn't have the time to wait for the next renegotiation period. So I laid all of my cards on the table and approached my boss, Principal Marilyn Highland. "What I really need is part-time hours with full-time benefits."

"No problem," she responded, "You'll still be a full-time employee. You'll just be absent a lot." Marilyn devised a plan in which she would hire for me my own personal substitute teacher. I could interview candidates and select someone I felt comfortable working with. Whenever I was away with Chris my sub would be there, so my class would essentially be taught by a two-person team. There would be consistency. I would work three days a week, have four days with Chris, and still maintain the medical coverage. Bobby, being self-employed, would work around my schedule. This began my long relationship with my teaching partner, Laurie Hayes.

At first I wasn't sure if this schedule would really work, but it did. Part of me wanted to chuck the whole thing and accept the devastating financial consequences—anything to be with my son. But the schedule gave me a sort of balance that I needed during those trying times. It got me away from the hospital a few days a week, and it gave my other two children a much-needed mom at home for a few days a week. It did the same for Bobby. It kept both of us from feeling overwhelmed, at least not at the same time, anyway.

But, no matter how well we planned our schedule, there always seemed to be another unexpected emergency around the corner.

September 18, 1997

Today we found out firsthand why they park the "crash cart" (the cart containing emergency meds) outside the room when administering certain drugs. Chris had a horrible reaction.

Bobby took him up earlier in the day for a scheduled ARA-C admission. Another chemo drug called L-asparaginase is also given during this phase of the treatment. It's an intramuscular (IM) leg shot. Chris and Bobby call it "L-asparagus."

I was still at home, but Bobby was with Chris. Bobby had gone across the street to RMH to sleep for the night. Between 11:00 PM and midnight Chris started getting hives all over his body, and he experienced tightness in his chest. First they gave him hydrocortisone and benadryl, but he only got worse. He didn't start to improve until they gave him epinephrine (adrenaline). This prevents respiratory distress ...

Both Bobby and I found all this out the following morning. We were furious that no one had called us. Apparently one of the nurses had asked Chris if he wanted them to call his dad and he'd said, "No, that's OK." They had exercised extremely poor judgment in letting a ten-year-old decide if his parents should be informed of a severe allergic reaction in progress. I was at home, but Bobby was only a few steps away. What if Chris had gone into terminal respiratory failure? Then it would have been too late to call us to his side.

That was typical of Chris to not want to wake up or worry his father. Later, he told me how scared he was. It brought tears to my eyes to think of him lying there alone covered with hives and struggling to breathe. I wondered how long it took for the nurses to even respond after he pushed the call button.

Up until then we felt that Chris was receiving excellent care, but this incident really shook us up. We made sure that Dr. Barbosa was made aware of it, and we heard lots of apologies, but now we felt that we couldn't let our guard down. It added even more weight to the enormous burden we were carrying. "We want to be notified if Chris so much as sprouts a funny-looking pimple!" I admonished.

As it turned out, they had responded quickly to his reaction, so his life was never really in danger; however, he suffered needless anxiety by not having us called. If I had to do it over again I would have written a carefully worded formal complaint. Although it may seem counterproductive to complain to the very same people you are trusting with your child's life, they are human and mistakes occur. In this case a written complaint would have gotten the attention of a department head who could have made sure that it was mandatory policy to notify parents immediately in such situations.

That same week we were offered tickets to the Bucs-Miami game at Hoolihan Stadium in Tampa. In addition to the tickets we would also be given the opportunity to appear on the "Jumbotron," the giant screen overlooking the field. The game was on Sunday so the big question was would we be able to get Chris out of the hospital on time? This became our focus for the week. It was a great distraction thinking about the game and our lovely mugs appearing on the massive screen. I asked Chris if he wanted me to make a banner for us to hold up, and he liked the idea. So I went to Joan, my favorite RMH volunteer, a sweet grandmotherly type who always carried a photo of her pet Chihuahua, and asked her for an old sheet and some markers. I made a huge banner that read "We Love the Nurses on 2 Southwest, From the Ditmars."

September 21, 1997

Chris ate a little bit of breakfast. He finished his chemo about 11:00 AM. He told Nurse Laurie that she looked like Princess Diana. She laughed and told him that sucking up wouldn't get him out any sooner.

We made it out in time to go to the game. Since we had an extra ticket we took Jasmine's dad, Tony. Chris really enjoyed his company. It was like having another kid with us. It was an exciting game—the final score was Bucs: thirty-one, Miami: twenty-one.

During the game Chris became a little nauseous so I took him to the first aid station to lie down for about fifteen or twenty minutes. After a while he felt better and was ready to return to the action. He amazes me.

The technicians had a predetermined time for us to appear on the Jumbotron. When they signaled us we jumped up and down on the seats and held up our banner. It seemed like the whole stadium was cheering for us. If they knew how brave Chris was, they would be. On the way home Tony hung out the window, cheering and hooting. I think Chris had more fun watching Tony than he did watching the game.

For a few brief hours all we had to worry about was the movement of a football up and down the field. Little escapes like that meant a lot to us. Many charitable organizations regularly donated tickets to sporting events to the hospital, the clinic, and The Ronald McDonald House. When caring for a chronically ill child sometimes parents are afraid to attend such events, but whenever Chris's counts weren't dangerously low we were encouraged to do as many normal activities as possible. It helps to have something to look forward to, a brief ascent on the roller coaster of chemotherapy.

That fall Bobby and I had settled into a routine, although you could hardly call it "routine." We usually scheduled Chris's hospital admissions on a Thursday, and Bobby would take him up. Chris would be seen in the clinic first then he'd be sent across the street to the hospital with his admission papers. Bobby would return to work in Sarasota on Friday, and then I would come up. Since my teaching days were Tuesday, Wednesday, and Thursday, I always had the long weekend to be with Chris. If Chris was well enough for visitors, we'd bring his brother and sister up for the weekend.

I was fortunate that my teaching partner, Laurie Hayes, was extremely competent as well as flexible. I made sure that all of my lesson plans for the upcoming week were completed by the time I left on Wednesday. Laurie was able to implement them, and make adjustments as needed. If an emergency arose she was "on call" to work in my classroom. Dr. Highland, our principal, also made sure that Laurie had as much work as she wanted in other classes on the days that I was there. She was Bay Haven's permanent substitute with my classroom as her priority.

The children settled well into the routine, and amazingly not one parent complained. We were a successful team, and our students' performance reflected this. It was also a blessing that I taught in such a unique school. Bay Haven School of Basics Plus is a magnet school, which draws students from all over the county. It is not a "district" school, although it is public. The program relies on strong family commitment to volunteerism and participation. Each family must sign a contract in which they agree to support the program. Students sign a contract to follow rules and do their homework. Parents agree to sign the homework nightly and participate in mandatory PTO meetings. There are also wonderful computer, music, and performing arts programs. As a result, Bay Haven has a waiting list of over three hundred to get in, and it boasts top test scores year after year.

What all of this meant to me was that we were "family," and the Bay Haven community took care of us. Chris was a fourth grader there when he was diagnosed, and I was a fourth-grade teacher. I remember standing up at our very first faculty meeting that year, announcing that my son had leukemia. Marilyn, Laurie, and I had met ahead of time and had worked out our schedule. When we shared our plan with the staff the outpouring of love and support brought tears to my eyes. Not one day went by that I didn't receive numerous hugs, prayers, and kind wishes. These were also accompanied by practical offers of help such as babysitting Jarrod, doing classroom errands, and cooking meals for us. After a month or so I stood up at another faculty meeting to thank everyone, and I added, "I never knew chicken could be cooked so many different ways!"

In the meantime I had met other parents up at the hospital who weren't as fortunate. One mother of a young cancer patient told me how her boss, a lawyer, had found a convenient excuse to let her go. Another lived too far from the hospital and had made the difficult choice to quit her job and rely on charity so that she could be with her child. A few families came from foreign countries and couldn't even speak English. I tried to imagine what it must be like trying to assimilate all that it took to care for a cancer patient, and have to deal with a language barrier as well. Many were single parents with other children who didn't have the luxury of a partner to share the burden. They had to leave each Monday and return to work, leaving their child behind in the hospital. Some children went days with no visitors or family by their side.

Looking around me and seeing all of this made me enormously grateful for the support that we had received. Our friends' and coworkers' attitudes had been, "How can we help?" not "Oh, I guess you're going to be gone a lot." Bob and I also had parents who lived nearby, and they frequently kept Jarrod overnight so that Bob and I could have some precious time alone together. Reflecting on this kept me from getting overly angry or feeling sorry for myself because it wasn't hard to find someone who was worse off.

Still, some anger was inevitable. All one had to do was look in the daily paper to see perfectly healthy individuals who were involved in violent crimes. Bob and I couldn't help but shake our heads and say, "Why couldn't that murderer get cancer instead of our wonderful little boy?" But there weren't any answers to our questions. There was no "Why." The experience definitely made us question our faith. Why would God allow such a terrible disease to inhabit the body of our innocent child?

In a conversation we had one day, Chris helped me find a partial answer. "Mom," he said, "why did God let me get cancer? What did I ever do to deserve this?"

"You didn't do anything to deserve it." I replied. "God didn't make the cancer happen. I think it's just something that happens in an imperfect world, like war and hunger. There're sweet little babies starving every day, and they sure don't deserve it either. I think when God gave us free will it meant that he wasn't going to stop all the bad stuff from happening."

"But why me?"

"I don't know, Chris. I wish I had the answers. But I do know one thing. You are very special, and very loved. God knows you are suffering, and I think he's saving you a very special place in Heaven. I think you will have a VIP seat."

"Do you think I'm going to die?"

"No, you're in remission. I think you'll get better, then help other kids like you."

"Cancer still sucks."

"Yeah, it sure does. But we'll be here with you every step of the way, buddy."

"I love you, Mom."

"I love you too, Chris, and I'm so proud of you."

It wasn't until I attempted to explain things to Chris that I actually started to sort them out in my own mind. Children have a habit of doing that—making us stretch beyond ourselves. That was one of my favorite reasons for being a teacher. I remember not having a clue about the difference between a solar eclipse and a lunar eclipse, until I had to teach it. Things always became so much clearer when you had to explain them to someone else. Of course, scientific concepts can be researched and proven. Spiritual matters can't, at least not on such an obvious level. But they can be thought about and discussed. One can decide what to believe and what not to believe. And that's what Chris and I did. We took a spiritual journey together.

Despite all the pain and fear that cancer brings, our family always knew that we were loved. The gentle touch of a nurse, a bear hug from a Ronald McDonald House volunteer, a basket of goodies on our doorstep, a kind letter, the caring faces of my students; all of these things wrapped around us like a warm homemade blanket. And sometimes late at night, when Chris was sleeping, and all was quiet except for the gentle growl of his infusion pump, I could almost feel the love around us. A few times I glanced upward almost expecting to see a guardian angel.

So that's what made our crazy schedule bearable. It was the love we found in each of the different places; home, school, and at the hospital. The love gave us hope. It gave us the strength we needed to operate in what seemed like a constant state of crisis.

October 16, 1997

Chris was up most of the night last night. He was not keeping down the tiny bit of food he ate, so we decided not to wait until Friday (his scheduled clinic day) to see the doctor. Bobby took him up there this morning and I went to work. We figured they would admit him so I packed him a bag. Sure enough, Bobby called me at work and said that they did admit Chris. He was anemic, had severe mucositis, and had a heart flow murmur. They said that the heart flow murmur would go away after he was hydrated again.

At first they thought he would be in the hospital for twenty-four hours, then they changed it to two to four days. He was put on morphine for pain.

That's the way it was with our "routine." We had to be prepared for anything. Side effects from the high doses of chemotherapy were all too frequent. Bobby and I were like two doctors who each had our "on call" days. We could pack in five minutes flat.

For the next two days Chris slept a lot, and received continuous IV fluids. The doctors decided to lower his dose of methotrexate (the drug that causes the mouth sores) by 25 percent. In addition to this they planned to increase his dosage of leucovorin, which is a rescue drug given just after the MTX. I had learned that the drug doses on the protocol weren't written in stone. There were therapeutic ranges. One had to stay above the lower limit to successfully keep the cancer at bay, but there was some leeway for children who were particularly sensitive to certain drugs. In Chris's case it was the MTX. I made notes to that effect in my journal. I would make certain his caretakers didn't forget.

4

WHAT ANGELS ARE MADE OF

October 19, 1997

This morning we read in the paper that Tanya McKenzie died. Yesterday when I saw Dina in the hall and waved I had no idea that Tanya was doing so poorly. They had a lot of visitors and now I know why. She died about 10:25 AM, the paper said. She was five years old. I remember how Dina comforted me last summer when Chris was first diagnosed. How I wish I could do something for her now. But, wow, she's done something for me. She's been kind and courageous. She's given me a new hero.

… Today was also the oncology unit's annual Halloween party at the Vinoy Hotel. Chris received a three-hour pass so we could all attend. Before we left the hospital we organized our costumes. Bobby put on a pair of "Spock"(pointed) ears. Every time a nurse walked into the room they had a good laugh. When Dr. Rossbach came in Chris took advantage of the distraction and blasted him with some spray alcohol. Chris had a "Dr. Pain" costume which consisted of a lab coat sprinkled with stage blood, Jarrod was a monster, and Erin wouldn't be caught dead dressing up so I told everyone she was dressed as an embarrassed teenager with an annoying family …

I dressed as Dr. Cone, the "conehead" doctor. For this getup I wore a large latex conehead, which resembled those worn by the alien characters famous from the movies and the Saturday Night Live TV show segments. Each year I resurrected my conehead from the attic when it was time for my fourth graders to study the solar system. I had practiced the signature monotone "conehead" speech and dressed in alien garb and presented myself to the class as an intergalactic substitute teacher. It had become an annual ritual that frequently coincided with Halloween. Therefore, it seemed logical that the conehead should make an appearance at the hospital, and at the children's party. To complete my attire I wore surgical scrubs decorated with planet stickers, a stethoscope, and carried a patient urinal, which doubled nicely as a drinking cup. As I was walking around I spotted a roll of stickers at the nurses' station that read "Medication added," so I peeled one off and plastered it onto my conehead.

... I had so much fun dressed as Dr. Cone that I decided to make rounds. This consisted of me entering the different children's rooms using my stethoscope to listen to their elbows. I then declared that their vital signs were excellent and held up a sheet of paper with pictures of road signs. Nurse Nancy, "Smelly Melly," turned down my offer of a free rectal exam. I commented to anyone who would listen that there was a beautiful Earth out last night ... I accomplished the impossible—I even embarrassed Chris. Of course that didn't stop him from loading apple juice in a syringe and squirting anyone unfortunate enough to get in range.

The Halloween party was impressive. It was in an air-conditioned tent with lots of food and a DJ. We saw the Wilsons and the McDonalds (Kevin and Brett's families) and we sat with Tony, Diana, Jasmine, and the rest of their family. The children all looked so wonderful in their costumes. It was easy to forget how sick many of them are. I dragged Dr. Rossbach out onto the dance floor to do the "Macarena" alien-style. For a while we all forgot about cancer until Chris tried to eat some candy, and his mouth sores hurt too much. What a strange day—full of both sorrow and laughter.

After the Halloween weekend at the hospital Chris got to go home for a few days, but he had to return on the twenty-fourth to stay on schedule. Usually we were able to squeeze in a couple of days at home where Chris could get out of the house and go to a movie or a restaurant. He had a tutor who came to the house twice a week. It was impossible for him to attend school with any regularity. Even on the days when his counts were high enough and he felt well enough (the two didn't necessarily happen at the same time) we spoiled him and let him do whatever he wanted. Looking back I am so glad that we did.

His first couple of days in the hospital were usually good ones as well, as it took a few days for the chemo to make him sick.

October 24, 1997

This is an ARA-C admit, so Chris won't have to deal with mouth sores. The hospital is crowded so we had to wait a while to get a room. That didn't matter because Jo Jo is here and he and Chris had a great time together playing Nintendo and doing all sorts of crafts. As a matter of fact, they got a little carried away and finger-painted the bedspread!

It started when Chris was sitting on Jo Jo's bed, and they accidentally spilled some paint on the bedspread. Well, it turned into a painting frenzy and they ended up painting the whole sheet. I thought it was really quite attractive, I mean, who am I to stifle creative genius? It looked like a Jackson Pollock painting. Jo Jo's dad, John Sr., was equally impressed. He hung it on the wall. We invited all the nurses in to see our brilliant children's first exhibition.

The following day, Bobby and I made the difficult decision to attend Tanya's funeral. We were both drawn to it, and repelled by it, but our desire to express love and support won out over our fear of facing the same future.

October 25, 1997

This morning Chris was happily playing video games with Jo Jo, so Bobby and I went to Tanya's funeral, which was close to the hospital. It was very moving and well-attended. I had the chance to hug Dina and tell her that Chris now has an extra angel looking out for him. She obviously had a large and loving family. I was glad that we could go and support them ... Tanya looked like a baby doll, the kind whose eyes close when you lay them down, beautiful, lifeless. I'm sure her family must have been thinking of the times when she was full of life, scampering between the pews.

That day made a huge impression on me because it was the first time we knew a child on treatment who had died. I wish I could say that it was to be an isolated incident, but that was not the case in the tough cancer-filled world we now inhabited. We looked at Tanya's parents with a mixture of awe and fear. They were living our worst nightmare, and they were doing it with dignity and courage. That night I added them to my prayer list, and they've been on it ever since. At the time I had no idea how long that list would become.

That admission for Chris and his subsequent recovery went well. ARA-C was almost always kinder to Chris's system than MTX. Chris was able to stay home for two weeks without any complications. His next scheduled admit was November 13.

November 13, 1997

It was pouring rain when Bobby drove Chris up to the clinic, so he dropped Chris off while he went to park. Meanwhile Chris walked in alone, and when the nurses asked him where his parents were he told them that he had ridden his bike! That would be quite a feat—riding forty miles or so from Sarasota, including the ride over the Sunshine Skyway Bridge.

Chris also had a fun day at the hospital. He and Jo Jo helped Ethan (a child-life counselor) run the video bingo game, and they were interviewed on Channel 9 News. They were doing a story about the hospital, so naturally the staff recommended that they vidoe tape the two resident characters, Chris and Jo Jo.

Jo Jo had been admitted a few hours before Chris, so he "saved" the bed next to him for Chris. To accomplish this he piled all of his clothes on the other bed, and told the nurses that no one else could have it but Chris. Foolishly, they actually attempted to place some other poor, unsuspecting child in that room, but were quickly rebuffed.

They started Chris's HDMTX about 5:00 PM. He's getting more fluids this time and 25 percent less MTX. Hopefully, this won't be as hard on him.

He threw up during the night, but was able to get back to sleep.

Video Bingo was a Thursday evening tradition at All Children's Hospital. The child-life therapists who run the children's activities had a little closed circuit TV system that enabled them to broadcast the game into all of the rooms. The patients were given bingo cards at their bedsides and were able to play by tuning into the designated channel. When they had "Bingo" they simply called a four-digit extension number and they could speak to the therapists. Winners got to see their names scrolled across the screen, and they were entered into a drawing for a grand prize, which was usually a popular toy or a large stuffed animal. At times the program could become rather dry, so Chris and Jo Jo often took it upon themselves to liven it up a bit.

Their favorite technique was to phone the extension, disguise their voices, and pretend to be about three years old. They would do this after only two or three numbers had been called so that it was impossible for anyone to have won. The conversation usually went like this:

"Hello, who's calling?"

"Hewo, I fink I gots bingo."

"Who is this?"

"It's Mikey, I'm free years old, and I fink I gots Bingo."

"Oh no, honey, it's too soon. Ask your mom to help you."

"What did I win?"

After the therapists had their number and knew it was their favorite prank-sters, they'd change their routine. It wasn't Thursday if Chris didn't call at least once and use his ET alien voice pretending that he was trying to "phone home," Naturally, I egged them on. This could be excellent training for careers in broad-casting, acting, stand-up comedy, or child therapist! I mean, who am I to stifle creative genius?

Many of the hospital days had a surreal quality about them, yo-yoing back and forth between sickness and playfulness.

November 14, 1997

Chris is feeling OK but is not interested in eating. He was scheduled for a spinal at 11:00 AM, but they were running late as usual. While we were waiting we went into the playroom and played Chutes and Ladders and Battleship with Kevin Wilson and his mom, Jane.

Jo Jo's mom, Anna, brought in some photos from Chris and Jo Jo's last hospitaliza-tion, when they had painted the bed. We have lots of other friends here, too: Diana and Jasmine, Brett McDonald, and his mom, Tara.

Tina told me that Brett has some mysterious spots in his bones around his pelvic area. They don't know what they are, and he's in a lot of pain.

Chris's spinal went OK, but when we returned to his room the smell of food made him throw up. A little later Chris felt better and we went to the child-life craft activity and made little magnet critters with Jo Jo and Kevin ...

... Later in the day, Brett felt better so Chris went over to his room and they played Nintendo together. While they played, Brian, Brett's dad, said that the dark spots were from bone that had died from Brett's radiation treatments.

When Chris was done playing with Brett the nurses asked him if he would mind showing his mediport to a newly diagnosed patient. As usual Chris was very obliging, and he even told her all about the flavored anesthesia they give you for the surgery.

After finishing his twenty-four-hour bag of HDMTX Chris got twenty minutes of IV 6mp which will be followed by six hours of IV 6 MP. Despite bouts of nausea Chris managed to play a game of Pictionary with Jo Jo and me.

At this point in Chris's treatment I could walk around the U-shaped hematol-ogy, oncology floor—2 Southwest, and recognize almost all of the children's names on the doorways. Most of them, like Chris, were regulars, which made 2 Southwest a community of sorts. Despite the circumstances, it had a comfortable familiarity, almost like a neighborhood, although it was a neighborhood with a high mortality rate. I didn't realize it at the time, but that day would be the last time we saw Brett.

November 15, 1997

Chris threw up some last night, but was able to get some sleep. When the nurse woke him up this morning he was disoriented and he asked her if it was Christmas. I guess

Christmas will never be quite the same for us any more. Our Christmas wish this year will be our son's survival.

... The mother of a patient who looked like he was three or four went ballistic today. Her son pulled his IV tubing out of his mediport, and she panicked. She was out in the hallway screaming and carrying on. The staff had to spend a lot of time and energy calming her down, explaining that it wasn't serious and he wasn't in pain. If she had just shut up and listened, they could have had the problem corrected sooner. They should have given her a shot of fentanyl! (Chris's favorite happy drug).

... Brett went home today, and the buzz on the floor is that his prognosis is grim. The nurses aren't allowed to say, but they can't stop the gossip ...

Jo Jo also went home today, so my strategy was to get Chris out of his room and distracted before he could start feeling sorry for himself with his two buddies gone. We ended up spending most of the afternoon in the room of a recently diagnosed patient named Michael Olsen. We had met them briefly a couple of weeks ago. It had been Michael's first admission and he was being prepared for the surgery to put in his port. As usual, the nurses asked Chris to show Michael his scar, and the small bump (the port is just below the skin) in his chest. Chris had done a superb job of putting him at ease, so now they were happy to see us again.

Michael had a new Playstation, so he and Chris enjoyed the video games. While the boys played I chatted with Michael's parents, Robert and Karen. I was amazed by how similar our families were. Michael was eleven, and Chris was ten. Just like Chris, Michael was the middle child with an older teenage sister and a younger brother. But unlike Chris, Michael had a more rare from of leukemia. His prognosis was not as good as Chris's.

I showed Karen my notebook and filled her in on as many positive things as I could think of. I told her about the wish organizations, the cancer camps, and The Ronald McDonald House. I had become one of the "experienced" ones. It felt good to help someone new.

Chris made it home on Sunday evening. That had definitely been his easiest MTX hospitalization so far. Unfortunately, we were only home a few days when we received some shattering news.

Almost all of my journal entries were made while I was in the hospital with Chris. The most obvious reason for this was that I needed to record vital medical information. The other reason was simple—that's when I had the time. While at home I was teaching school and caring for my other two children. During the work week I barely had enough time to go to the bathroom, much less write in my journal. But on Monday the twenty-fourth I made a rare home entry in my log.

November 24, 1997

Chris was sitting next to me at the kitchen table when the phone rang. It was Anna, Jo Jo's mom. She told me that Michael Olsen had died! Apparently he had contracted an infection and had died very suddenly. They called it septic shock. In his immunio-suppressed body the infection had spread so rapidly that there wasn't anything they could do. We were stunned.

Chris and I cried most of the day. He asked me if I thought he was going to die like Michael. I tried to comfort Chris by telling him that Michael's leukemia was a differ-ent type, and Michael had not achieved remission.

I called Karen, and I can't really remember saying much besides "I'm sorry." I kept thinking about how we had spent hours in Michael's hospital room the week before. We had talked about getting all of our kids together, and having Michael and Chris go to camp together. We had looked at a cell diagram and compared our sons' leuke-mias. Karen had told me that prior to his diagnosis, Michael had displayed almost no symptoms. His leukemia had been discovered when he had gone to the dentist to have a tooth extracted and they couldn't control the bleeding. And now he was gone, just like that.

Michael's sudden demise was a sober reminder of how important infection control is during chemotherapy. It is the reason chemotherapy patients must be admitted for antibiotics and observation at the first sign of a fever.

Michael was also the first friend that Chris lost. Tanya was much younger, and not a playmate of his, so her death didn't have nearly impact on him that Michael's did. Michael's death generated many conversations about angels.

November 28, 1997

This admit is for ARA-C, vincristine, and daunomycine. Chris is scheduled to get three twenty-four-hour bags of ARA-C. It's not the high dose ARA-C, so we are hoping for a smooth weekend.

Kevin Wilson has been here all week for a fever, and is getting ready to go home. His mom, Jane, and I talked softly about Michael's death when the boys weren't lis-tening. Kevin doesn't know yet.

After they left Chris brought up the subject of Michael's passing. Intuitively, he had known what we were talking about, and he had had the sense not to mention it in front of Kevin, who is a little younger.

"Mom, do you think Michael's in Heaven?"

"Oh, absolutely," I replied.

"Do you think he's an angel?"

"Yes, I do, Chris, I think he's a special angel in charge of kids with cancer. I think he's a guardian angel looking out for you."

"Yeah, I think so, too. They need angels that know their way around the hospital. Mom, what do you think Heaven's like? Do you think it's clouds and stuff? That would be cool if Michael were bouncing on clouds."

"I think Heaven is a little different for each person," I'd theorized. "I think it's filled with each person's favorite things. When I go to Heaven there's going to be a giant ski mountain with spring weather, no lift lines, and perfect conditions."

"I think Michael's up there playing Nintendo." Chris had responded.

Previously I had never given guardian angels much thought. I had always believed in them, not just because I was Catholic, but also because the idea seemed very logical to me. I could never really explain it, but I had always had this peculiar, yet comforting, feeling that my paternal grandmother, Nana, and my mother's Aunt Margaret were watching over me. Both had died when I was in my teens, but I had gotten to know them well enough to get a sense of their spirits.

Nana was probably the most unselfish person I had ever met. After raising four children of her own she helped raise my two cousins when their mother left them at a very early age. Her parents had emigrated from Ireland, and although she had never set foot in the country, they had instilled in her a rich love of Ireland, its music, and recipes. Nana baked Irish soda bread and loved nothing more than seeing the grandchildren eat it up along with a big plate of ice cream. If there was no ice cream in the house, she always gave us money and sent us to the corner store.

My fondest memory of Nana is when were all up in the mountains of Pennsylvania visiting with my Aunt Mary Rita (who was Nana's daughter and my dad's sister) and Uncle Paul. They had a home by a lovely lake, and we often enjoyed water skiing behind their boat. One summer day we all coaxed Nana to come down to the dock to watch us ski. She was quite large and slow moving, so it was a challenge for her to negotiate the rocky path down to the water's edge. She finally nestled herself into a folding chair, delighted to watch our youthful fun. When my brother, Tim, got up on his skis and waved to her she started laughing and waving back. Suddenly, the chair fell over into the bushes behind her, leaving her stranded on her back. While most elderly folks would probably have become completely flustered, Nana laughed even harder. She was the one who taught me the importance of being able to laugh at myself.

And my Great-aunt Margaret, she taught me that a really good angel probably has just a little bit of devil in her. I remember one evening long ago sitting around our dining room table, being politely bored as my parents entertained a room full of grown-ups. The discussion had turned to books and recent best sellers. While my very Catholic great-aunts, some of whom were nuns, were all clucking their tongues and shaking their heads at the deterioration of society's morals, Aunt Margaret leaned over and whispered in my ear. "Well, honey, I prefer the dirty novels myself."

So when Chris and I sat there in his hospital room imagining angels, I thought of my deceased relatives watching over us. They are not pure, porcelain statue-type angels, but beings with grit and humor. Angels of a God who would allow Nintendo, skiing, and maybe even steamy paperbacks, in their Heavenly domain. I thought of all the religions around the world and their various beliefs from incarnation to ancestor worship. I figured that they all had a little glimpse of one much larger truth. For the most part we were clueless as to what that truth was, but it wasn't hard to believe someone was up there pulling for us. That someone may as well be people we knew. It made perfect sense to us that God would assign newly deceased children to look after the ones on Earth. When discussing these issues with Chris I definitely had to shoot from the hip, but I knew that reinforcing his faith was more important than theological accuracy. We had been thrust into a frightening life and death situation, so we explored the boundaries of our faith together.

November 28 cont'd

Chaplain Peter stopped by and played Nintendo with Chris for a while, but he was no match for Chris. He only lasted a few minutes in each game before Chris killed him. Later, about 5:00 PM Chris threw up so he was given some benadryl for the nausea. The benadryl put him to sleep.

In the meantime, Bobby stayed with Chris while Andrea, one of the nurses, and I tried to go to Michael's viewing, but after driving around for an hour and a half we got completely lost and had to give up.

While we were gone there was another death on the floor. Bobby reported that little Tanisha, who had been a good friend to Tanya, passed away about 6:30 PM. The two little girls had undergone their bone marrow transplants at almost the same time, and had kept each other company in the isolation of the bone marrow unit.

There was a lot crying and loud mourning from the family members, and the staff cleared the hallways. Bobby peeked out of the window in Chris's door and watched as they removed Tanisha. He said that they put the body under the gurney with sheets draped over the sides. That way it appeared that the gurney was empty. Now we know why you never see a body in the hospital.

November 29, 1997

Chris slept well last night and is feeling better this morning.

All of this death is really getting to me. It has to be affecting Chris, too. When Dr. Grana examined Chris this morning I asked her to hook us up with some long-term survivors that she might know. She suggested that we ask Julie at the clinic. That's where the survivors go for their follow up exams.

Michael's funeral is today, but I'm not going to risk getting lost again. However, I've been thinking about them and praying for them all day.

Chris and Jarrod had fun together in the playroom. It's so wonderful when Chris feels well enough to play with his little brother!

After the playroom, Chris, Jarrod, and little Josh, a tumor patient, all had fun blowing bubbles at the nurses' station. The nurses have all adopted Jarrod as their official helper. He told me proudly that he "works with them." Chris's room is right across from the nurses' station and I could see the top of Jarrod's little head going back and forth as the nurses gave him important things to carry. He was also in charge of telling them when the phone was ringing or when a patient had pushed his bedside call button, which makes a beeping sound.

November 30, 1997

Today, Ethan from child-life showed Chris his album of pictures from ROCK Camp. ROCK is an acronym for Reaching Out to Cancer Kids. It's a camp near Orlando, and Chris will be invited to go there for a week next summer. It looks absolutely beautiful, and Chris is excited about it. They also made a moving turtle out of a bowl, a dowel, wheels, a rubber band, string, and toothpicks ...

Chris continued to do well and was able to go home the following day. The hospital wasn't a bad place to stay if one felt well enough to enjoy the games and crafts; that is, if you didn't mind the fact that children died there.

5

A TRUE FRIEND

December was a good month for us. A good month for a cancer patient means that side effects are minimal, there are opportunities to do some normal activities, and there are no unscheduled hospital visits.

We took nothing for granted and seized every opportunity for fun. If Chris felt well enough, he and Bob loved going to the movies. They often went to matinees to avoid crowds and germs. That was often followed by lunch at Chris's favorite restaurant, The Old Salty Dog. This is a rustic waterfront restaurant with a lovely view and outdoor tables (another plus for avoiding infection). If Chris was too lethargic or if his counts were too low, we would rent videos and games. Many of our friends and family had responded to our suggestion to buy Chris video rental coupons, so we saved a lot of money.

Some of Chris's hair had grown back so he didn't look quite so obvious, although it was still quite thin. Children sometimes stared or pointed, and I knew it hurt Chris, but he handled it beautifully. Usually he'd lean over and whisper in my ear, "Kids, if only they knew what it was like!" Chris could always take a negative situation and make a humorous comment. The cancer had seemed to make him grow up so suddenly.

But he was still a little boy, and he longed to do little boy things. Once an avid soccer player and an agile tree climber, his physical energy was completely sapped. He missed those things and would often remark how he couldn't wait for all of this to be over with so he could resume the activities he'd lost.

He also lost friends. Cancer did that. It weeded out the true friends from the fair weather friends. Chris had two very special friends; one stayed by him, but the other one all but vanished.

Tommy (name changed) had been Chris's best friend since they were four years old. Our two families were very compatible, and had spent many Sundays together on the beach. Tommy and Chris built sandcastles with elaborate roadways full of Matchbox cars. They splashed in the water and clambered over the

rock jetty together. Tommy lived a few blocks away and he and Chris were insep-
arable. Even after Tommy's family moved to a new neighborhood they kept in
touch, until the cancer came.

Tommy's parents were among the first people we called with the news of
Chris's leukemia. "He'll be in the hospital a lot," we'd said, "it would mean a lot
to him to have Tommy come and visit." But as the months of treatment wore on,
Tommy never came to visit. It wasn't really Tommy that had let Chris down; it
was his parents. We found out later that they never even told him Chris had cancer—at least, not until more than a year later, when they had no choice.

Paul was Chris's other buddy. They met in second grade when I started teaching at Bay Haven and Chris began attending there. Paul and Chris were in the
same third- and fourth-grade classrooms. They shared a love of animals, building
with Lego bricks, and anything related to the "Star Wars" movies. They did
school projects together and often hung out in my classroom after school, first
finishing their homework, then watching a movie or playing on the computers.
Paul was a bit of a free spirit and occasionally got himself in trouble, but Chris
seemed to have a calming influence on him. Paul was sharp and often helped
Chris with his math. They were good for each other.

When Paul found out Chris had cancer he was devastated, but unlike
Tommy's overprotective parents, Paul's parents gave truthful answers to his questions. Paul lived right across the street from Bay Haven so he often stopped by
my classroom to get progress reports on Chris. It was difficult for Paul to visit
Chris in the hospital, because his parents were divorced and his father, whom he
lived with during the week, didn't drive. I gave him the toll-free number to All
Children's Hospital, and he called Chris frequently. If Chris wasn't well enough
to chat on the phone Paul had no problem speaking with whomever was with
Chris. I thought he showed a lot of initiative and compassion for a ten-year-old.

Whenever Chris was well enough we'd have Paul over for a visit or an overnight
stay. While most of his other friends forgot about him, Paul helped fill the void.
The buddy "Paul-Bo," as no comprehension of the limitations of a chemotherapy
patient, so we'd have to explain to them why Chris couldn't attend birthday parties
and get-togethers. After a while the invitations stopped coming, but his teachers at
Bay Haven made sure that Chris had a steady stream of cards and letters. Chris was
never the type of person who needed a lot of friends; he always preferred quality to
quantity. So with his buddy "Paul-Bo" as Chris called him, and us at his side, Chris
had a tolerable month. The only glitch was when his counts didn't recover in time
for us to schedule his next admission when we would have liked to. This meant that
being home for Christmas was questionable.

December 22, 1997

Chris is in for HDMTX. He was scheduled for last Thursday, but was not admitted because his counts were too low. Our goal is to get Chris in and out by Christmas Eve. It's going to be close.

… About 11:00 AM Nurse Sonya told us that his chemo was ready but they would have to run bicarb fluids through his system first. This will raise his urine ph level (it must be within a certain range before chemo can start) and enable him to get the MTX out of his system more easily.

We had fun shooting darts at our homemade target range that we set up on the shelves. Cups are one point, socks two points, and Winnie the Pooh is four points. The toy dart gun was a Christmas present that I let Chris open early … Tony is here with Jasmine and he came into the room to play with Chris. They added little NFL action figures to the target range and had a jolly time.

When we grew tired of that game we amused ourselves with Chris's sticky coin. This is a fifty-cent piece with mounting tape on the back of it. The tape makes it nearly impossible to pick up. We placed it on the floor in the hallway just outside Chris's room and watched people try to pick it up. I suggested that we turn it into a science project to determine whether more males or females went for it. What can I say? Once a teacher, always a teacher. However, this proved difficult to determine since there are a lot more female staff members. Anyway, we had a few laughs.

… Later that evening Chris was antsy and couldn't sleep. So we decided to go for a walk across the bridge that separates the hospital from the outpatient medical building. To our surprise we found the medical building unlocked. This proved too irresistible, so we decided to see how much trouble we could get into. We were quite the pair, with Chris pushing his IV pole with one hand, and clutching his dart gun with the other. We wandered around for a while, and then Chris spotted a cockroach on the wall in one of the waiting rooms. "Hasta la vista, Baby," Chris said, aiming his dart gun at the bug. The cockroach proved harder to hit than originally anticipated, so we ended up taking turns to see who could nail the little sucker first. Chris finally hit, and we left the squirming critter belly-up on the floor.

"I wish the prize was no more cancer." Chris commented as we headed back to the hospital.

In the few weeks since Chris's last hospital visit I heard that Brett McDonald had died. One of the nurses at the clinic told me, and I just didn't have the heart to tell Chris so soon after Michael's death. Unfortunately we didn't find out in time to go to his memorial service. It seemed like death was closing in all around us. I continued my search for long-term survivors, and I continued participating in as many silly antics as possible. The nearness of death made us even more determined than ever to *carpe diem* (seize the day).

December 23, 1997

With Chris's approval I have selected a pair of my most tacky earrings to present to Smelly Melly as a Christmas gift. They are truly ugly, even by my standards. I think that the original intent of the designer was to make them look like snowmen, but they're kind of lumpy and distorted, and they look like they were accidentally left in the microwave. In addition, they are hideously large. This makes them the ideal gift to annoy Nancy.

"Oh, Smelly Melly, we have a present for you!" Chris chirped as we handed her the box.

"I'm not sure it's safe to open anything from you Ditmars people." Nancy has this great way of wrinkling up her nose when she says our name. "Oh God, what are these things?"

"They're snowmen, of course. Can't you tell?"

"No, not really. You don't actually expect me to wear these, do you?"

"Of course we do!" Chris insisted, "That way people won't notice your face so much!"

My sentiments exactly.

December 24, 1997

… I should have known better than to try and shield Chris from Brett's death. He heard the nurses talking, and he figured it out. We discussed it, and he didn't seem to take it as hard each other on Earth, I guess that was because Chris saw that Brett was suffering. He looked so thin and pale the last time we saw him.

We talked some more about angels and Heaven. Chris and I concluded that because Michael and Brett had known each other on Earth, and they had both died of leukemia, they were definitely together in Heaven. "I guess I have two guardian angels now, Mom. Michael has someone to play Nintendo with."

Using his own special brand of adolescent philosophy, Chris had surmised that Michael and Brett's common suffering had destined them to be together in the hereafter. He had identified them as kindred souls, bound together to play for all of eternity. Furthermore, Chris drew comfort from this viewpoint, and considered his deceased friends as ever-present angels. During those special conversations I knew that I had always been destined to be Chris's mother, and for that I was filled with tears of gratitude.

That year I got the best Christmas present a mother could ask for; Chris made it home at 6:00 PM on Christmas Eve.

6

THE END OF INPATIENT

January 3, 1998

We came in for a scheduled HDARA-C admit. Ole' Smelly Melly is the charge nurse and actually took care of us by giving Chris a private room. Deep down, way way deep, we know she loves us.

Jarrod, as usual, charmed all of the nurses and was following Nurse Andrea around. Chaplain Paul showed up with a loaded syringe (full of water), and this somehow evolved into an all-out water battle. Nancy produced an extra-large syringe and shot straight into our room from the nurses' station. She nailed me right in the head. I wonder, do they teach that at nursing school? Chris and I decided to play dirty and we filled our syringes with grape juice. We even talked poor, innocent Andrea into participating. We launched an all-out assault on the nurses' station. Poor Andrea ended up crouching behind the desk while Chris climbed over the counter and shot from above. Even Erin got in on it and shot a few people. Jarrod was running around squealing with delight. At one point, Nancy was chasing me down the hall with a cup full of water. (Wouldn't that have been a great time for one of those tours they give to the financial supporters to walk through?) Finally, someone yelled that a supervisor was coming, so we all grabbed towels and started mopping up the floors.

Just as all of this craziness ended the Bushner family showed up. I had contacted them through an organization called Candlelighters, which assists families dealing with cancer. They had exactly what we needed to see at that time—a child who was a long-term ALL survivor. The parents were named Clair and Vince, and their son Vince Jr., twelve, was a ten-year survivor. Like Chris he also had a fourteen-year-old sister.

We had a wonderful visit and talked about the ups and downs of drug reactions, fear of relapse, finances, and the effects of having a child with cancer on the siblings. Young Vince has a completely normal life now. After all of the death we've seen, this was just what the doctor ordered.

... Later, while I was over at RMH eating dinner I heard that Nancy and Andrea returned to Chris's room to seek their revenge for the earlier water battle. They tried to smear some chocolate cookies on his face, but he dumped his milk all over Nancy. I guess milk and cookies go together. Imagine those nasty nurses picking on my pure and innocent child!

Around 6:30 PM Chris started feeling nauseous, and that was the end of the fun times for this day. At 8:30 PM he threw up and had a nose-bleed at the same time. He got sick again at 10:30 PM, but was able to go to sleep after receiving some antinausea meds.

Until that visit from the Bushner family, patients who had survived more than five years with ALL pre-B (Chris's form of leukemia) were just phantom statistics. It seemed like we had been immersed in a world of death, and I remember Bobby and I saying to each other, "So where is that 75 to 80 percent that supposedly survive? All we see are kids dropping like flies." Meeting a real family that had a child who was cured meant the world to us. I think that it meant even more to Bobby and myself than it did to Chris, because he trusted us so much. When we told him he was going to live, he believed us. But we needed our hope replenished so we could keep up the energy that it required to pass it on to Chris.

It took a bit of digging and a number of phone calls to arrange to have that family come and visit us. The meeting occurred only because I was assertive and persistent, qualities that many overburdened parents of children with cancer may not possess. Looking back on the experience I now realize that hospitals and support organizations aren't doing enough to match long-term survivors with the newly diagnosed patients. I feel that this should be just as much a part of the treatment as the drugs. A little bit of hope goes a long way.

Chris continued to feel miserable for the remainder of that admission. He didn't eat or drink, but continued to receive IV fluids. I was glad that we had carried out our big water battle when we had the chance. Those antics took the place of boyhood activities that Chris could no longer enjoy. Being able to laugh and play were simple pleasures that most families with healthy children take for granted. Those small doses of fun and mayhem helped contribute to Chris's positive attitude.

Once he got home Chris started eating again, and he had no more unscheduled hospital stays. We now had only two admissions remaining in Chris's inpatient protocol!

January 22, 1998

Bobby brought Chris up for his HDMTX hospitalization. His hemoglobin (red cell count) was only 6.9, so he needed a transfusion of packed red cells before he could begin his chemo. He also had a spinal.

For bingo tonight Chris felt pretty energetic so he went up to the third floor where they broadcast the game. That way he could participate and be on camera. Bobby reported that Kevin, Jo Jo, and their favorite child-life counselor, Ethan, were all there so they had a grand old time. Chris enjoyed answering the phones when the patients with bingo called in. He used his perkiest game show host voice, and also did his famous "ET" impersonation upon request. You've never heard "Bingo" until you've heard "ET" say "Bingo." And, boy, do those patients pay attention when ET calls the numbers!

January 23, 1999

I came up this morning and Bobby went home. I brought Chris a can of Silly String and he immediately draped the entire room in it. There were bright green strands everywhere on the walls, the ceiling, the bedrails, and the clock. He used up the whole can at once.

We had a fun afternoon playing computer in the school room, and enjoying some board games …

… About 9:30 PM Chris's twenty-four-hour bag of HDMTX was just finishing and he got sick. I stayed with him until his stomach settled down and he was asleep for the night.

When I stayed up at the hospital with Chris I had an established routine. I would stay with him in the room until he was asleep, or was comfortable enough to allow me to go across the street to the RMH to get some sleep. If he was very nauseous or running a high fever, I stayed with him in the room. This meant sleeping in a comfortable chair that converted nicely into an uncomfortable bed. That combined with the IV meds that were programmed to beep rather loudly when the infusions were complete, the flood of white light from the hallway every time the door was opened, and the fact that there was often a roommate who may also have a parent in the room, meant very little privacy and even less sleep. Of course, the roommate's pump would also beep at intervals that always coincided with that exact moment you thought you might actually be dozing off.

Needless to say, I sought refuge in a cozy room at The Ronald McDonald House whenever possible. Each of the rooms had a phone with direct access to the hospital, so that the nurses or Chris only had to dial a four-digit extension to summon me. There was also a security van that could drive you after hours. That meant you could be in your child's room at a moment's notice, and it relieved some of the guilt I felt when I didn't sleep in Chris's room.

My morning routine often included a run around the hospital. I had been an avid jogger for years, and I continued this practice when I was up in St. Petersburg. Once I had gotten past those first few traumatic weeks I had decided that I needed to continue running in order to hang onto what was left of my sanity. Typically Chris slept in until about nine thirty or ten o'clock, so this gave me ample time to run three or four miles, take a shower, and get up to his room before he missed me. If he woke up before I got up to his room he could call my extension and leave a message so I knew that he was awake and waiting for me. The exercise-induced endorphins gave me the courage to face the long days at his bedside. The running also helped burn off calories that might have turned to fat sitting around all day in a hospital room. Also, I knew that I could be a better caretaker for Chris if I took care of myself.

January 24, 1998

I went for a run then came over to Chris's room about 9:30 AM. I felt energized, and skipped the elevator, taking the stairs two at a time. He was just waking up and feeling OK. Bobby, Erin, and Jarrod arrived around 10:30. Along with Kevin they all played video games together and had a good time.

Mimi and Pop (Bob's parents) visited for a while. It was very pleasant because Chris felt fine. Erin went back to Sarasota with Mimi and Pop … It was a good day. Chris only threw up once …

Chris went home the following day. That left only one more hospitalization!

February 4, 1998

This is Chris's last scheduled chemotherapy hospitalization! It is the end of his consolidation therapy. From here, we move on to two years of outpatient maintenance. Chris will receive a lot of chemo and have a lot of tests. He will get three twenty-four-hour bags of ARA-C, along with L-ASP, vincristine, and daunomycine. He will also get an electrocardiogram to make sure that the chemo hasn't damaged his heart.

… Despite the fact that Chris threw up twice this evening, he's in good spirits because he knows this is his last admit.

I was back in Sarasota working when Bobby brought Chris in. The night before Bobby and I had written down all of our questions about the transition from consolidation to maintenance. We had a lot of them, and there was also the fear that with less chemo going into his body, Chris would relapse. So it was with mixed feelings that we moved onto the next phase of Chris's treatment. We knew that those drugs had kept his cancer at bay. We were a little apprehensive about leaving the security of the hospital and its powerful drugs.

February 5, 1998

Bobby asked Dr. Rossbach today if he thought that we should keep Chris's mediport in during maintenance. Dr. Rossbach said that there were pros and cons. The mediports sometimes got infected, but leaving his in meant that Chris would not have to get stuck for his weekly CBCs (Complete Blood Counts), and his spinal taps (which are still required during maintenance). Chris could still play sports with the mediport in. Sports-related injuries to the ports were rare. So Dr. Rossbach was basically leaving that decision up to us.

Bobby and I asked Chris how he felt about it. He wanted the port out and said, he wouldn't mind the weekly sticks. He wanted to be as normal as possible. We couldn't blame him.

Bobby also met with Nurse Julie about our list of questions. She explained his new drug schedule, which basically consisted of two chemo drugs, the 6 MP pills, and once a week leg shots of MTX. In addition to those drugs he will be on several prophylactics such as antibiotics and antifungals. We would also have antinausea meds available ...

The idea behind maintenance is to prevent the cancer from returning, but to allow the patient as normal a life as possible. The longer Chris maintained his remission the greater his chances of survival. The first year was important, but he wouldn't be considered fully cured until he had passed the five-year mark. We were told that most relapses occur when the patient is completely done with maintenance and off all drugs. However, Chris had an excellent chance of never relapsing. At least we felt somewhat safe about the next two years, but we still had a long road ahead of us.

Friday, February 6, 1998

I came up after school, and Chris and Bobby told me how much fun Chris had on the hospital bingo show last night. He answered the phones and sang their corny bingo song. He also entertained the viewers with his impersonations. I wish I could have been there.

He had a good day today, and once again the staff called upon him to comfort a newly diagnosed patient who was facing the mediport surgery. I was so proud of him ...

Saturday, February 7, 1998

This will most likely be our last full day here. Chris should clear his MTX level tonight or tomorrow. I didn't sleep well last night. I kept thinking about Brett McDonald, who relapsed right after his consolidation. The medi-vac helicopters landing and taking off kept waking me up. They were an eerie reminder of how precarious life can be.

I arrived from RMH around 9:30 AM. The weekend manager, Bill, had cooked us a big breakfast. Chris woke up when I came into the room, and he was in good spirits.

... Dr. Rossbach came by. He seemed very positive about Chris going into maintenance and said that his prognosis remains good.

We entertained ourselves for a while by squirting Smelly Melly with a watergun filled with orange juice and water. Nancy snatched Chris's watergun, but I got it back and squirted her in the butt. "Well, it's the biggest target in town!" we told her. When she finally made it back to the nurses' station Chris called her and disguised his voice. He told her that he was James Bond ...

I have such mixed feelings about leaving this place. I sure won't miss seeing Chris vomit, and get mouth sores and leg pains from that high dose chemo, but I'm scared that the lower drug doses on maintenance might allow his leukemia to return.

Oddly, I'm going to miss this place. I feel like we have so many friends here. It's become a second home to us. I'll miss the nurses, and I'll especially miss teasing Smelly Melly. I'll miss the staff and volunteers at RMH: all the girls: Carla, Judy, Donna, and grandmotherly Joan. I'll miss big Bill, the kindhearted cooker of chili. When he knew we were staying at the house he often brought us homemade sausage.

I think we'll always stay connected somehow, maybe through return visits or volunteer work. I recently heard about an organization called Team in Training for Leukemia. You sign up for a marathon and fund-raise in honor of a patient. That might be a neat way for me to use my running to help make a difference. Anyway, we'll still be visiting the clinic here every week for two more years ...

On Sunday we walked out of 2 Southwest for what we thought was the last time.

After a round of hugs and good luck wishes, we moved on to the next part of Chris's journey.

PART II
REMISSION: 1998–1999

7

THE GIFT OF REMISSION

We had finally made it to maintenance. Now if someone said, "Get a life!" We could respond "OK."

While the treatment process so far had been long and arduous, now that consolidation was really over it seemed like it had gone by quickly. I don't know if it's one's memory or time itself that plays that trick, but my mother always used to say, "If you think time goes by fast now, wait until you get older, it only gets worse."

But time was now our greatest gift. With Chris on much lower doses of chemotherapy he was free to go back to school and resume normal activities. The doctors gave him carte blanche to participate in whatever activities he felt up to. He would continue to get weekly CBCs to make sure his counts were OK, but no major drops were expected. This meant we had our boy back!

We really didn't have our old life back; however, we were changed forever. We were still living with a life-threatening illness, and this made us grateful for any day that brought normalcy. Simple routines like getting the kids up for school and listening to them argue over whose turn it was in the bathroom were like gifts from Heaven. Driving to Bay Haven with Chris at my side again was better than winning the lottery.

Chris gradually regained energy, but he was still somewhat compromised. The 6 MP pills upset his stomach, and the weekly MTX shots made his skin itch. He still didn't have the stamina for an entire physical education class, but he could participate on a limited basis, and then sit out when he was winded. If a full school day was too much for him as well, Bobby would pick him up at lunchtime.

Of course Chris would talk him into going to the The Old Salty Dog for his favorite clam chowder. Those were precious father-son afternoons together. Bobby and I would lie in bed at night and he'd tell me about his lunch with Chris. "He's such a neat kid. He has all the waitresses charmed." Bobby would say.

"He's just like his old man," I'd reply.

At Bay Haven Chris was cared for by the entire school. I kept snacks in my classroom for him to munch on when his stomach was upset, and I had a sofa in my reading corner. His teachers allowed him to visit me whenever he asked. He'd wander in and say, "Hi, Mom," choose a snack from my closet, then sprawl out on the sofa. My class would usually greet him with a "Hi, Chris," then they'd go back to work. Chris never took advantage of the situation, and usually after fifteen or twenty minutes he was ready to return to his own classroom.

Naturally, my fourth-grade students were curious about Chris's condition, so I taught them about cancer. Since leukemia is cancer of the blood I began by teaching them about the three main types of blood cells: red cells, white cells, and platelets. I explained that the red cells carried oxygen throughout the body. The white cells fought infection, and the platelets would clot at the site of an injury in order to prevent excess bleeding. It was a certain type of mutated or changed white cell that kept reproducing uncontrollably that created leukemia. That was followed by an explanation of chemotherapy and other related concepts such as remission and relapse.

They asked detailed, thoughtful questions, and I answered in kind. I have no doubt that my students ended up knowing more about cancer than many adults. Along the way I had the opportunity to explain that Chris had required blood transfusions to replace his red cells and platelets that had been depleted by the chemotherapy. "Tell your parents that donating blood helps cancer patients," I reminded them. "And don't ever tease kids who are bald or look different." One day it dawned on me that I wasn't just teaching them about cancer, I was teaching them to be compassionate. And Chris was teaching them about courage.

In March of that year Chris and I received an invitation to travel to Park City, Utah. My mother, my Aunt Mary Rita, and a group of skiers were renting some slope side condos for a week. Mom and Mary Rita had an extra bedroom in their condo, so they asked me if Chris and I would care to join them. My first reaction was that it would be too much for Chris, but Bob suggested that I ask the doctors first.

So we checked with them before mentioning it to Chris, and to my pleasant surprise, they had no problem with it. They would schedule his shots around the trip. Chris and I were ecstatic. Mary Rita mailed us a trail map and we pored over it like two kids in a candy store. Chris had always been my soul mate when it came to snow skiing. During our annual trips up north I had introduced Erin to the sport but she had never caught the "bug" like Chris did. Even when he made the switch from skiing to snowboarding it didn't affect the fun we shared together. Chris was comfortable on almost any terrain, and I had been an avid skier since I was a teenager, so we loved nothing more than exploring the trails together.

Bobby wasn't much of a skier, either. However, he knew how much I enjoyed it, and unselfishly he had always been supportive of this rather expensive hobby. In the nineteen years that we had been married he had made sure that I had the opportunity to ski each year. Sometimes he came along, but more often than not he put me on a plane and said, "Have fun." I used to joke that I had made him sign a prenuptial agreement with an annual ski clause before allowing him to marry me and take me away to Florida. Usually my trips took me to the relatively tame mountains of Pennsylvania since that was where my family owned property. Anytime I had the opportunity to ski the Rockies was a real treat, and this time I was thrilled to be able to include Chris, who had never been out west.

Despite the doctors' OK, I was still a little nervous about taking Chris on such a big trip with his diminished energy level, but his enthusiasm won me over. "Mom, don't worry. If I get tired our condo's right there on the slopes. I'll be able to stop and go inside whenever I feel like it."

When we left I didn't know it at the time, but we were about to create one of the best memories of my life. From the moment the in-flight movie ended and Chris pulled up the window shade and got his first glimpse of the snow-covered peaks, he was in awe. "Wow, look at that," he grinned. "That's where I'll be boarding!"

My apprehension returned when the shuttle dropped us off outside our condo which was at an elevation of about nine thousand feet. "Wait up, Mom, I need to catch my breath." Chris was unable to make it across the parking lot without stopping to rest.

"What have I done?" I thought. "I've dragged my son across the country up into this thin air, and his doctors are two thousand miles away."

But my fears were soon laid to rest. By the following day Chris had adjusted to the altitude. Mom and Mary Rita joined us, and for a week we played in a winter wonderland.

Most mornings Chris either took a snowboard lesson or played in the snowboard park, which was a special slope set aside for boarders. It had little jumps and half pipes. Some of the teenage boarders who were with our group took Chris under their wing and showed him around the area. Meanwhile I would head to the top and blast through as many runs as I could, catching my breath on the chairlifts, grateful for the fact that I was a runner and in fairly good shape. Then, later in the morning Chris and I would hook up and ski together for the rest of the day, either by ourselves or with Mom and Mary Rita. We'd stop at the condo for lunch or when Chris needed a rest, but he amazed me because he didn't need to stop for very long.

That week Chris and I enjoyed that special bond nourished by sharing an activity that we both loved. We carved our way down the mountain making *S*s, taking turns following each other. We chatted on the chairlift, breathing in the cold mountain air, and pointing with glee when we spotted an enormous porcupine sitting in the branch of a pine tree.

Since Park City had night skiing we even tried that. After dinner, Chris and I would head out the door for hour or so while Mom and Mary Rita declared us "crazy." We'd stay out until we couldn't stand the cold any longer then tumble into bed enjoying a healthy kind of exhaustion, ready to start over again in the morning.

I think when we look back upon our favorite memories in life it's not the days or weeks that we remember, but the moments. It was near the end of the week, on a day that started out poorly, that I had one such instance. I could live to be 112 and win a Nobel Prize, but I know I will never value anything above that special moment on the mountain with my son.

Chris had gone off to the snowboard slope while I took a guided ski tour of the mountain. Our guide gave us a history of the Park City area and pointed out the entrances to the old silver mines as we skied by. It was both educational and exhilarating. But when I arrived at our designated meeting place, Chris wasn't there. Instead, Mom and Mary Rita were waiting. "Chris fell, and he's hurt. It's not serious, but he's asking for you. He's back at the condo."

I raced back to the condo, feeling guilty for having so much fun and leaving him alone. When I got there Chris was lying on the couch. "Mom, my back hurts. I don't want to go boarding any more." He explained that another boarder had hit him from behind and had accidentally run over him. His back had a long scratch on it, but I couldn't see any other injuries. I made sure that he could move everything, and he assured me that it was only the sore on his back that hurt. He seemed more shook up than anything else. Relieved that his injuries were minor I resigned myself to an afternoon of watching TV, but then, the snow started falling.

It was a gentle, windless snow shower with big meandering flakes—the kind of snowfall they made Christmas cards from. It was so serene that it seemed as if the whole mountain was whispering. "Chris, come out and play."

I coaxed. "Forget about boarding, we'll just catch some flakes on our tongues." This proved too irresistible to my Florida boy.

First, we dove backward into the fresh powder, flapping our arms and legs, making snow angels. Then came the obligatory snowball fight in which I was pelted mercilessly. Chris took no prisoners. I ran into the locker room in the lower level of the condo to escape the onslaught, and that's when I spotted the sleds. Stacked in a corner was a pile of round disks. "Chris, c'mere, let's go sledding!"

By now it was late afternoon and the ski slope closest to our condo was closed. That meant we could sled down the hill without worrying about skiers running into us. We each grabbed a round sled and trekked up the hill. We then hopped on, and soared down. If we tucked our legs under Indian style we could almost fly. By sticking our legs out we could easily slow down. Spinning was another giddy option. We did this repeatedly until we were breathless and exhausted. Finally, we sat poised at the crest of the hill ready for our final ride. We watched in awe as the sun set on the Wasatch Mountains, the shadows creeping slowly upward from the valleys below. The peaks were bathed in sparkling pastel shades. It occurred to me that the view before us was exactly like my description of Heaven. Then Chris turned to me and said, "I'm so glad you're my mom."

I think that the ski trip helped to build Chris's confidence. He had to rediscover what it meant to be a regular kid again. By then his hair had grown in thick once again and he looked wonderful, but best of all, he no longer looked different. He signed up to play spring soccer, and I explained the situation to his coach. The coach had to be alerted to look for any unusual bruising or bleeding. Chris would need more frequent rest periods than most of the players, but otherwise he was treated just like the others, and that's exactly the way Chris wanted it.

"Mom, don't go telling the whole world I have leukemia, OK? If I think they need to know, I'll tell them."

We respected his wishes, and we trusted him to self-monitor regarding his physical exertion. Chris had shown excellent judgment during his physical education classes at Bay Haven, sitting out when it was too much, but participating whenever he was able. He could have very easily taken the "poor me" approach, especially with his mom being a teacher, but he never did. His teachers and coaches regularly reported that Chris interacted in a friendly, outgoing manner, and never drew inappropriate attention to himself when he was resting, although he was occasionally guilty of performing some of the same silly antics (such as doing impersonations) that he had done in the hospital.

That spring Bob and I signed up to do a marathon with Team in Training for Leukemia. TNT is the main fund-raising organization for The Leukemia Society of America (which has since been renamed The Leukemia and Lymphoma Society). I had heard about the organization while up in St. Petersburg. They recruit ordinary people to train for a marathon or distance event, and to raise funds for cancer research. In return for the running and fund-raising commitment, TNT provides the athlete with expert coaching, organized training events, and they pay for the transportation and the lodging at the marathon.

Team in Training books travel and lodging at group rates and keeps the overhead low so that 75 percent of the money raised goes directly to research and patient aid. I was captivated by the idea of using my running to make a difference. I thought of all of those mornings jogging around the hospital while Chris was inside, and now I had the chance to convert that energy into research dollars. That, combined with the fact that completing a marathon was on my "things to do before I die" list, made the whole thing completely irresistible. Of course, I hoped that it wasn't on my "things to do **right** before I die" list.

I chose the Dublin City Marathon in Dublin, Ireland. I did this for two reasons; being of Irish descent, I felt that the saints and my ancestors (especially Nana and Great-aunt Margaret) would protect me along the way. And being a teacher, I had the summer off to train for a fall marathon (it was in October). When I informed Bob that I had committed to this marathon he informed me that I should be committed. "You're going to train for a marathon?" he said, "You don't even have time to clean the house."

"Well, honey, do you think if I don't do this marathon our house is going to be any cleaner?" He knew he was licked so he did what all the best husbands do—he signed up too.

That began a new mission for us—fund-raising. The minimum requirement for Dublin was $4,500.00 each. That meant that Bob and I had to raise $9,000.00. We tackled the challenge with energy and enthusiasm. After all, we had our very own poster child. Our attitude was that after what we had been through, who could turn us down?

I began by writing letters to everyone I had ever known, wanted to know, or whose name sounded even vaguely familiar. This included over two hundred of my dearest friends whose addresses I obtained from the School Board personnel directory.

Bob took advantage of his business contacts whenever possible. He recruited several area restaurants to display donation jars, but his best contact was with a local travel agent. For years Bob's company, Globe Painting, had painted the travel agency's offices, so he knew the owner quite well. We were thrilled when they donated a cruise for us to raffle. Naturally, Bob convinced a local printer to donate the raffle tickets. We never went anywhere without tickets in hand, so we were constantly selling chances. Whenever anyone asked how Chris was doing or if there was anything they could do, that became our cue to whip out a book of tickets and ask them how many they would like. After a while I think some of my friends and colleagues began hiding when they saw me approach.

While many of the TNT runners lamented that the fund-raising was tougher than the running, we thrived on it. Raising money for research gave us a focus and a purpose. For the past year we had stood by helplessly as our Chris battled cancer, and now we finally felt as if we could do something. It was exhilarating. We were also extremely grateful that Chris was in remission, and it gave us a chance to give back.

It also gave us a chance to educate our friends about cancer issues. We updated them on Chris's progress, and we quoted the statistics that we had learned along the way. Each week nearly two thousand Americans are diagnosed with a blood-related cancer, and every nine minutes another patient dies. Despite this, the research money had made a huge difference, because thirty years ago a leukemia diagnosis was a death sentence, and now the cure rate was over 75 percent. We reminded everyone that their contributions were making a difference.

For the most part, it was a good summer. Chris had the opportunity to attend the ROCK (Reaching Out to Cancer Kids) camp. It had absolutely everything you'd wish for at a camp, boating, crafts, campfires, archery, horseback riding, and a beautiful setting. There was also a trained medical staff. It was a wonderful CP (Cancer Perk).

My sister, Maureen, who lives in New Jersey where we grew up, threw a big block party, which served as both a fund-raiser and a family reunion. I had the opportunity to connect with cousins that I hadn't seen in a long time. Maureen had obtained an impressive collection of goodie baskets donated by local merchants. These were raffled off for the cause. It was a wonderful celebration of survival, family closeness, and working together for the cause.

But a few days before Chris's birthday in June we received some devastating news. Jo Jo had died. Out of all of his hospital friends, Chris had been the closest to Jo Jo. They had shared a humorous way of coping with their cancer. Jo Jo was often a coconspirator when Chris pulled his pranks. His death hurt even more than the losses of Michael and Brett. His death also brought back all of our fears.

"I don't know why I bother making friends at the hospital," Chris said tearfully. "They all die."

This was followed by more discussions of Heaven and angels. Once again Chris had to grapple with looming death and lost friends. While most children his age had nothing more traumatic to deal with than broken bones or getting on the same baseball team as their friends, Chris was left to wonder if the cancerous shadow of death was coming for him next.

"You're in remission," I reminded him. "And besides, Jo Jo had Ewing's Sarcoma. That's a completely different kind of cancer than leukemia."

I wondered how much more loss Chris could stand. I wondered why God had chosen me to be the mother of a child with a life-threatening illness. I prayed that I was up to the task.

And once again, in the midst of the fear and anguish, Chris showed his amazing spirit. When I got on the phone with Jo Jo's mom, Anna, Chris asked to speak to her. He told her how much he missed Jo Jo. He let her cry in his ear.

It didn't take long for Chris to assimilate Jo Jo into his vision of the Heavenly ranks. He now had three personal guardian angels, working a special cancer assignment.

"Do you think they hear me when I talk to them, Mom?"

"Yes, I do, Chris."

"How come they can't answer?"

"I don't know, honey. I've often wondered that myself. Maybe if people on Earth were allowed to have conversations with angels in Heaven we wouldn't pay enough attention to all of the stuff we have to do while we're here. Maybe God wants to see how we do on our own. But that doesn't mean we're alone. I think you should talk to Jo Jo, Michael, and Brett whenever you feel like it."

"OK, Mom, I will."

I have very few regrets in my life. When faced with tough choices I've always tried to make the best decisions based on the knowledge I had at the time. But I regret not making the trip across state to Jo Jo's funeral. I regret not giving Chris the choice of attending, and most likely it would have been too difficult for him, but I wished that I had been there. Later, Anna described the service to me. Jo Jo's dad was a fireman, so all of the county fire trucks had lined up for his funeral procession. What a wonderful way to send a little boy to Heaven.

In the meantime, The Suncoast Children's Dream Foundation contacted us. They had arranged for us to go on the Disney Cruise at Christmas time. So we moved past our fear into the anticipation of a wonderful trip. Such was the rollercoaster of cancer.

By the time fall arrived we had surpassed our fund-raising goal for Team in Training for Leukemia by $4,000.00. We had raised a total of $13,000.00! Now we had both the marathon and the cruise to look forward to.

During that time Chris had begun making appearances as a patient ambassador for The Leukemia Society of America. This involved attending meetings and banquets and having his picture taken with the marathoners. Even though Chris sometimes didn't feel like going, he always rose to the occasion. He chatted with the athletes and smiled for the cameras. He was a natural.

As the marathon approached, Bob and I received an invitation to visit some friends while we were in Ireland. We had become acquainted with Damien and Catherine White of Roscrea, Ireland, through an online pen pal project that I had involved my class in. A mutual friend had given me Damien's e-mail address when I had inquired about the possibility of my class sending electronic mail to another class overseas.

For the past eighteen months my fourth-grade students and Damien's fourth and fifth class at the Corville School in Roscrea had been corresponding. Damien and I had matched each of our students with an e-mail pal. They had sent each other letters discussing birthdays, siblings, movie stars, music, and just about any subject that would interest a ten-year-old. Through the correspondence we had enjoyed comparing currencies, holidays, and especially sports. We learned that an Irish pound was a measure of wealth, not weight, "football" in Ireland was really soccer, and "hurling" was a favorite sport played with a stick, not a slang expression for someone who was vomiting.

So when Damien and Catherine heard that Bob and I would be running the Dublin City Marathon, they extended us an invitation to visit. Their whole town was praying for Chris, they told us, and we knew that they meant it. It would be our first trip to Ireland, but we would have friends there cheering for us.

The marathon was an amazing experience—not just because of the physical accomplishment of propelling one's body nonstop for 26.2 miles, but because it offered us the wonderful opportunity to connect with so many different people. From the time we boarded our transatlantic flight in Newark and discovered that the plane was full of fellow marathoners from all over the United States to the time we returned home, we felt almost like missionaries preaching to the world to stay involved in finding a cure.

Bob and I traveled alone. We had offered the trip to our older two, Erin and Chris, and they had declined. Chris declared that long plane rides were only worth it if you got to go snowboarding. Erin didn't want to miss school, and besides, Ireland had a serious lack of shopping malls. My parents generously offered to babysit so Bob and I found ourselves in the delightful position of traveling kid-free. It would prove to be a wonderful, romantic respite after the trying year we'd had.

The biggest adjustment for us was the weather. After training in the Florida heat, the wind, rain, and mid-thirty degree temperatures were a challenge. I had always been told that cool weather was better than heat for marathon running, but I couldn't help but wonder where beneficial cool ended and muscle cramping cold began. I think it was somewhere on O'Connell Street.

On Sunday, October 25, the day before the marathon, we participated in the two-mile International Breakfast Run. This was a fun run for all of the non-Irish participants. It was followed by a breakfast and a T-shirt exchange. Hundreds of runners brought T-shirts from races all over the world to swap.

The atmosphere was fun and chaotic—like a cross between an auction and the floor of the New York Stock Exchange. Runners held up their shirts and an announcer called out where they were from. Whoever wanted it waved the shirts that they were willing to trade. I had brought about ten shirts from Sarasota to trade and I ended up with an interesting assortment from all over the United States and Europe. Later, these would become prizes for my fourth-grade students who researched facts about their locations.

That evening we attended the Team in Training pasta party. No marathon would be complete without the traditional carbo-loading ritual the night before. It was held in an enormous hall owned by The Royal Dublin Society, a traditional philanthropic organization.

The speakers included leukemia survivors and family members with heartwarming and inspirational stories. Bobby and I received recognition for being parents running in honor of a child with leukemia, and also for raising over $13,000.00 for cancer research. In all, the Dublin Marathon Team in Training participants had raised $2.5 million!

We felt incredibly proud and grateful to be a part of it all. Looking around that banquet hall, seeing hundreds of runners who had all dedicated themselves to saving children like Chris, gave me an indescribable feeling. There was a lot of love and hope in that room. It would serve us well the following day.

The marathon began in the heart of the Dublin downtown, on O'Connell Street. The temperature hovered in the high 30s and low 40s, but it was windy. This made it seem even colder. Just before the start I enjoyed the warmth of the huddle and the air of anticipation. All of the TNT runners wore distinctive purple singlets, and we chatted among ourselves, sharing our individual stories of those we knew with cancer. Bob and I each wore a picture of Chris pinned to the front of our singlets. On the back we were labeled as well. I wore a sign that read "Hi, I'm Maribeth from Sarasota, FL, U.S.A." I was ready to have fun.

The Irish spectators lined the course, clapping and shouting encouragement. The children were enjoying what they called a bank holiday, no school, and they were playing and running alongside us. Thanks to my sign, I heard frequent shouts of "Well done, Maribeth!"

After eight or nine miles we left the city and headed out toward the suburbs. I saw rows of colorful townhouses with brightly painted doors and tidy little gardens. Many families stood in front of their homes waving and cheering. Little Irish ladies had card tables set up along the roadside with water, tea, cookies, candy, or juice. Their red-cheeked children stood by the road with their hands stretched out to slap us a high five. Also plentiful were the TNT supporters waving banners with the purple and green logo.

After fifteen miles the wind and cold took its toll and my left calf muscle went into a spasm and said, "I quit!" but the rest of my body wouldn't let it. If Chris could endure all of the chemotherapy I could complete this marathon. I ran to make his pain my pain. I prayed that somehow my marathon effort would guarantee his continued remission. Maybe God could hear me best when I was out of breath.

Eventually the course wound back into the city, and although I didn't realize my hopes of breaking five hours, I did achieve my primary goal: finish vertical and conscious.

Along the route I had chatted with runners from around the globe, and that day the world was a small and wonderful place indeed. "I'll be praying for your son," many had declared after seeing Chris's picture on my shirt. By the time I crossed that glorious finish line adorned with its arch of colorful balloons, I felt as if I had collected prayers from all over the world.

Bob, who prior to our training hadn't run a step since high school, finished only about ten minutes behind me. And his experience was also rich and spiritual like mine. He reported similar feelings of camaraderie and achievement. When we found each other at the finish line we embraced. But our biggest hug was yet to come.

After another day enjoying the pubs and friendly crowds in Dublin we rented a tiny little Nissan Micra and headed cross-country to visit Damien and Catherine. Despite getting a bit confused on some of the roundabouts (traffic circles) we managed to find our way across the beautiful rolling countryside. We passed cows and sheep grazing beside rambling stone fences and tiny little villages with names like "Kinnegad" and "Tullormore." No matter how small the towns were they each had at least one pub. This was my kind of country.

After about two and a half hours we arrived in Birr, our rendezvous point with the Whites. It was a quaint little town with a roundabout in the center surrounded by colorful shops. Catherine met us there and we followed her to their lovely country home. After relaxing a bit and enjoying some coffee and cake we were ready to visit Damien at the Corville School. Finally, we would meet the children who had been corresponding with my students!

We traveled south about ten minutes to the town of Roscrea in County Tipperary. The Corville School is a one story stone building surrounded by farmland. The children in the schoolyard waved as we pulled up. They wore neat little blue uniforms, and some of the boys had on ties. Damien, who did double duty as both teacher and principal, greeted us as the front door. As we entered I noticed a banner written in Gaelic, and leaning alongside it was a pile of hurling sticks.

It was an unforgettable afternoon. Damien was quite excited to have us, and we visited every classroom. As we entered each class the children stood and sang a special Irish greeting song. We were also bombarded with questions: How many students at your school? How long is your school day? Do you all eat lunch at the same time? Do you have recess? Have you seen any movie stars? What movies do you like? Do you have your own computer? Were you married proper? When your students misbehave how do you punish them? But most touching of all were the questions about Chris: What kind of Nintendo games does Chris have? How is Chris doing? They all knew about Chris, and they were all praying for him.

I had brought letters and photos from my students, and I gave these out to their e-mail pen pals. Bobby had brought an assortment of hats with logos from baseball and football teams. He gave these to Damien to distribute later. But we weren't prepared for the special surprise that the students had for us.

Damien led us to the all-purpose room, which served as a lunchroom and an assembly hall. There we watched as the entire student body filed in, all ninety-three of them, for a very special presentation. One of the students came forward and presented us with a check for leukemia research! Before our arrival the entire student body had held a rummage sale to raise money in Chris's honor. It was very fortunate that Bob was operating the camcorder at that moment, for my eyes were quite filled up with tears.

After the assembly the older children were eager to show us their athletic skills. We went outside to their playing field, which was surrounded by pastureland, and they demonstrated hurling and Gaelic football. Hurling sticks resemble hockey sticks, but the part that hits the ball is larger. The rules allow the players to fling the ball in the air or hit it along the ground. The ball looked a little like a baseball, but it was very hard. The children wore helmets that resembled the type worn by baseball catchers. Gaelic football is like a cross between soccer and hockey. Some body contact is allowed, and both girls and boys played. Bobby and I videotaped the action, and I told the class how much my students back home would enjoy watching it.

Before we left Birr we went to the local bank to exchange the check for American currency. When we walked in Catherine introduced us to the teller as her American friends, and before we could say a word her face lit up and she asked, "How is your son?"

It was a moving experience to visit the land of my ancestors and be received by an entire town that was praying for our son. We had spent nearly six months training and fund-raising, getting ready for this trip, yet somehow we had managed to receive even more than we had given. Perhaps that was the greatest CP (Cancer Perk) of all.

Life continued in an almost normal pattern. Chris had occasional bouts of fatigue and nausea from the low dose chemotherapy, but the symptoms were much milder than they had been when he was on the high doses. He had his mediport removed, and he now had a full head of hair. He felt a part of mainstream life again, but with one important difference. He appreciated everything so much more. We all did.

We still had the ordinary family squabbles and trying times. Jarrod still tried to invade Chris's room, and Chris would still slam the door in his face and scream "Get out!" But now a day never passed that didn't include the phrase "I love you." Many times Chris was the one to say it first.

He had acquired a keen sense of fellowship. I suppose it was always there, for even when Chris was a small child he was personable. But now he seemed to relish the common everyday interactions such as making popcorn and watching a movie, or sitting on the sofa having his back scratched. Relationships were now even more important to him. When Jarrod wasn't being a pest Chris taught him his secret handshake, the one he and Paul had invented. He also sought out his big sister, often charming her friends into taking him to the movies with them. Even Erin had to grudgingly admit that the teenagers didn't mind having Chris around.

As the holidays approached we enjoyed looking at the brochure for the Disney Cruise. It was a four-day Bahamas trip that concluded on Christmas Day. About two years earlier, right after he stopped believing in Santa, Chris had started a special Christmas Eve tradition. It consisted of Chris lurking in the yard right outside Jarrod's window ringing a string of sleigh bells. Then Chris would quickly sneak back into the house and ask Jarrod, "Did you hear that? That's the reindeer flying overhead. They're getting ready to land so you'd better hurry up and go to sleep!" If anyone dared to try and give him away he'd smile and whisper, "Don't spoil the magic." We'd chuckle as Jarrod dove under the covers and did his utmost to fall instantly asleep. So of course, Chris hid the strand of sleigh bells in a corner of his suitcase.

The cruise was wonderful and relaxing, but the greatest gift was just being together as a family doing something different. I think Jarrod enjoyed it the most. He scampered from one activity to the next, hugging Mickey and dancing with the Chipmunks. The ship had three swimming pools. One was shaped like Mickey's head, and it had a huge curving slide that dumped the rider into Mickey's left ear. And of course, the Disney Magic cruised directly beneath the path of Santa's reindeer, and by golly, you could hear those sleigh bells!

Our year had certainly ended much better than it had begun.

We began the New Year by watching the Disney Marathon in Orlando. I had several friends and acquaintances who were running it for leukemia just as Bob and I had done in Dublin. Since Chris had not accompanied us on that trip we wanted to give him an idea what the marathon experience was all about. We also wanted to support our friends.

We stood by the roadside as thousands of marathoners ran by, hundreds of them, purple-clad leukemia runners who were giving their all for the cure. Chris was able to see the sweat and determination of the runners and they were able to see a brave young survivor cheering for them. Despite very cold, windy, conditions there was a wonderful sense of warmth.

As the morning wore on the weather deteriorated and grew even colder, but Chris never complained. I believe that he was connecting in a way far beyond his tender years. He was seeing people suffer through a grueling endurance event in order to prevent the suffering of cancer victims. He didn't verbalize this, but his cooperative attitude spoke volumes. He was doing what some adults never did—he was seeing the big picture.

Chris did something else that winter that surprised us. He asked to be retained in fifth grade. In my eighteen years of being a teacher I had never once had a student who asked to repeat a grade. Now my own son was making that request. Did he know something that we didn't?

In a way, I think he did. After his long absence from school the previous year he'd had no trouble catching up in reading, but math was a major struggle. He'd always had a mild learning disability that made memorizing the multiplication facts extremely difficult, but when allowed the crutch of a multiplication chart he was able to grasp all the concepts and successfully tackle computations involving long division and fractions. But now he couldn't even accomplish that. He was forgetting how to perform tasks that he'd previously mastered.

This frightened Bob and me, and we mentioned it during one of Chris's weekly clinic visits. At first the doctors brushed it off and told us to give him time, but he showed no improvement. He had become so frustrated in his fifth-grade math class that we made the difficult decision to send him to a fourth-grade class for math. Fortunately, the Bay Haven teachers handled it with their usual sensitivity, and Chris never felt ridiculed or teased.

But even the fourth-grade curriculum proved challenging for Chris. We felt that the matter required more investigation. So we repeated our concerns, and Dr. Barbosa ordered an MRI of Chris's brain.

It confirmed our suspicions. There was some dead brain matter. The chemotherapy had killed some of Chris's brain cells. "Leukoencetholopathy" they called it. It meant white (or dead) brain matter. Dr. Barbosa explained that the spinal chemotherapy, the same drugs that had been injected to prevent leukemia relapse in the brain, had indeed attacked some of Chris's healthy brain cells. The affected area was small, they assured us, and he would most likely learn to compensate, but it would never heal. The only thing that they could do was to discontinue the methotrexate they were giving Chris in his spinals, and hope that the damage didn't get any worse.

So we had a label, but not much of a solution. But even that helped because we could reassure Chris that he wasn't "stupid." He had never been a strong math student, and the chemo had hit him in his weak spot.

It's hard to sit in a doctor's office and listen to him discuss your child's brain cells. It's not the same as the other side effects like the mouth sores; those eventually went away. These were cells in Chris's head that were lost forever. Nobody, not even the best specialist, could tell us what to expect. Did they represent lost thoughts? Did it mean he'd never progress in math or would he just be inconvenienced and have to rely more heavily on calculators? What if the damage spread and affected his personality—his wonderful Chrisness?

"We'll have to do repeat MRIs every six months to make sure it's not getting worse," they told us.

I found that somewhat ironic considering the fact that we had to pester them to do the test in the first place. I asked them to tell me about other cases that they knew of.

"Well, most of the time we don't diagnose leukoencetholopathy until the patient has seizures. Before that, there are usually no symptoms."

When I heard that I didn't know whether to be relieved or frightened. Maybe both. We had caught it while the damage was relatively minor, but if brain cells continued to die Chris could end up having seizures as well. Now we had more delightful side effects to worry about. At least he was alive, and still in remission.

And amazingly, it had been Chris who had alerted us. He had known that some things weren't coming as easily to him as they should have. It made me realize that patients have a relationship with their bodies, not just their doctors. Sometimes the former speaks up before the latter. This wouldn't be the first time that Chris would knew something before the doctors (and we) did.

We told Chris that if he still felt this strongly about wanting to repeat fifth grade by springtime, we would agree. Another important consideration was the fact that Chris would have to attend a different school in sixth grade. Bay Haven only went up to fifth grade. If he wished to remain in Bay Haven's nurturing environment for another year, who could blame him?

Fortunately subsequent MRIs showed no further damage. Chris didn't let the math thing get to him, and Bobby promised him that when he grew up he could hire a foxy accountant to take care of business.

There was never any doubt whatsoever that Chris's personality wasn't impaired in the least. Chris was developing several interests that kept him happily occupied. He had always been clever with his hands and he had become an avid Lego builder. He was fond of purchasing kits for building space ships and elaborate jungle scenes. Sometimes after building according to the directions he would take his creations apart and change them around. The practical joker in him loved gags and magic tricks, so he also began collecting an assortment of those items as well.

In the meantime we lived as if every month was our last. We've all heard that famous question: "What would you do if you only had six months left to live?" That question takes on a whole new meaning when you are living with cancer. Bobby shared special lunches with Chris, and often took the boys to the movies. In March I took Chris out west again to ski.

This time we went to Heavenly Valley, which is a beautiful resort that straddles the California–Nevada border and overlooks Lake Tahoe. Once again, it wasn't just the skiing that we enjoyed, but the special time alone together. We stayed in a hotel in Reno that had a casino and a nightly magic show. Our first night there we went to the magic show and Chris was captivated. We had the opportunity to talk to the magician after the show, and by the second night Chris had worked his usual charm, and for the remainder of our stay the staff let him attend the show for free. Chris purchased a magic kit and began testing his tricks on me. Some were rather obvious, but I thought a couple of them were quite clever. This led to a scheme that we tried out in a restaurant the following evening.

One of the tricks was a tiny weighted bottle that lay on its side when the weight was inside. Without the weight it stood upright and could not be made to stay on its side. Chris bet our waiter a free round of drinks that he couldn't tip the bottle on its side. Chris first demonstrated how easy it was then, as he handed the waiter the bottle, he discreetly slipped the tiny weight out into his hand. The result was a free drink and a good laugh!

Besides enjoying the breathtaking view at Heavenly Valley we hopped on buses and tried several other resorts around the Lake Tahoe area. The rides were scenic and interesting, as the drivers would fill us in on local history as we drove along the lakefront. On the day we rode up to Kirkwood our bus driver was very knowledgeable about local Indians. He played Native American music as we wound our way through snowy valleys and past tribal battlegrounds. Instead of asking "Are we there yet?" as many kids would, Chris allowed himself to be tuned into the beauty and serenity of our surroundings. We gazed contentedly out the window as the rhythms of the drums washed over us.

That week we enjoyed one fabulous day after another. From the sun-drenched bowls at Squaw to the woodsy trails at Heavenly where you could ski across the state line, we played. We lived. We made more treasured memories. Those happy days were a great gift.

While the ski trip was a wonderful experience, if you asked Chris what the best thing about being in remission was he'd probably talk about being able to handle his pets once again. While he was on treatment and his counts were low we didn't let him near any animals except the dog, but a major part of Chris's childhood had been his love of animals. He'd owned an assortment of pets including our loveable black lab, Moonshine, a succession of hamsters and gerbils, all named "Max," and his latest pet, a Quaker parrot named "Kiwi." Chris had taught the bird several phrases such as "Hello," and "Hi, Chris," but Kiwi's real claim to fame was as the captain of Chris's remote control boat. Chris had taught the bird to perch atop the boat while he maneuvered it around our swimming pool. That was how the bird became known as "Captain Kiwi."

Chris was endlessly patient with his critters and would play with them and talk to them for hours. He would change his voice and pretend they were talking back to him (except for Kiwi, of course, who could speak for himself). One time Chris had a book report to do and the main character was a mouse, so he had his gerbil Max play the part. We video-taped various scenes from the book starring Max as the mouse with Chris doing the voice-over. In one scene from the book the mouse drives a toy motorcycle off the edge of a nightstand and falls into a trash can. So we placed Max on a table next to a toy motorcycle and taped him as he sniffed and wandered around the bike. In the background you can hear Chris speaking in a squeaky falsetto voice, "Oh boy, look at that bike. I think I'm going to ride it!" Then through the magic of video we made it appear as if the mouse and the motorcycle had fallen into the trash can. Of course the appropriate dialogue followed. I laughed until tears came to my eyes.

Chris also began volunteering at a local pet store. He wasn't old enough to obtain a paying position, but he figured by volunteering and getting to know the procedures they would hire him when he was older. I was impressed by his initiative.

Chris had an affinity for wild animals as well. He was always catching frogs and snakes. He'd look at them for a while then let them go. We researched local poisonous snakes, but not being an expert, I was still nervous. "If you have to touch snakes just catch the black racers," I'd say.

"Oh, the black erasers," Chris would respond jokingly. That's what he'd called them when he was younger.

I remember one time when Chris was about nine I glanced out of my kitchen window just in time to see him zooming down the street on a skateboard. One outstretched arm grasped Moonshine's leash as he was being towed. In his other hand he held a squirming snake. That vision of boyhood abandon is forever etched in my memory. It would have made an excellent Norman Rockwell painting.

Chris had always had a fearless sense of adventure, and during those months of remission when he was feeling well, it returned. It brought tears of gratitude to my eyes to see him wandering about the yard scooping up lizards and showing them to his awestruck little brother.

As a matter of fact, my favorite animal antic of his involved lizards. Chris would capture two lizards and hold them up to his ear lobes. Instinctively they would latch on and dangle like a pair of earrings. This always went over big when we had company, especially guests from out of state who weren't accustomed to Florida's plentiful lizard population.

That summer we snake-sat a cornsnake that belonged to Jarrod's kindergarten teacher. Chris kept the snake in his room, and enjoyed studying it. He'd lie flat on the floor, peering into the terrarium. We'd purchase mice to feed him, and as the snake gulped the mouse Chris would provide commentary, pretending to be Steve Irwin, the well-known host of the TV show "The Crocodile Hunter." Chris's Aussie accent was very authentic sounding, "Aww right now, 'ee's got'em. It's quite dangerous ..."

Of course at night when we said our prayers they had to include all of the animals: our dog, the bird, the snake, and every rodent Chris had ever owned. "... and God bless, Max, and Max, and Max, and Max, and Max ..." Also, we never forgot to pray for all of the kids in the hospital.

8

FAMILY

One of the hardest things about having a child with a serious illness is having other children who don't. All too often Chris was the center of attention. Erin was fourteen when Chris was first diagnosed so she spent a large portion of her teen years seeing him in the limelight. He continued to have opportunities to make appearances as a guest of honor at cancer fund-raisers and charity events. One time he was flown up to Baltimore as a special guest of a baseball team. Another time he got to sit on the bench at a basketball game with The Harlem Globetrotters. Erin was invited to most of these events, but she often declined to attend. Even though she was at an age where children typically begin separating from their families, she must have resented the attention Chris received.

I think most people assumed it was harder for Jarrod than it was for Erin, because they figured that she was old enough to understand; but I think it was the other way around. Jarrod was only three years old when Chris was diagnosed. He never knew anything different. Seeing Mom and Dad go back and forth to the hospital with Chris was normal for him. He also derived a lot of pleasure from attending some of the cancer-related events, which often had entertainment for children. On the other hand, Erin missed parties or sometimes had to stay with boring grandparents while we up at the hospital.

We couldn't change things, but we did our best to reassure Erin that we loved her. We told her over and over again that we would do the same things for her if she were sick. Unfortunately life isn't fair and Chris was the one who needed us the most. Yes, he was the one who always got the cards and gifts in the mail, but he would trade every single one of them in a heartbeat to be free of cancer forever.

Teenagers are a strange species. Their newly erupting hormones swing their moods like a pendulum. Combining that with a family dealing with cancer makes for some challenging moments. One thing Bob and I tried never to do was to compare our children, at least not to their faces, anyway. After all, how can you compete with a hero? That's what Chris had become. Likewise we never assumed that just because Erin now had the body of an adult she was bound to think like one. More often than not, the opposite was true. We saw a lot of childish pouting and temper tantrums.

"I hate you!" was flung at us on more than one occasion.

Depending on how my day was going I usually had one of two responses: "Well, I love you," or "Go to your room!"

It's easy to feel guilty for spending more time with your sick child. It's easy to feel guilty for thinking, "Well, maybe I really do love Chris more." But then I realized that it wasn't that I loved him more, it was just that life's circumstances had given me more time with Chris—more opportunities to talk about angels and Heaven, more chances to witness his bravery.

One thing I learned for certain. You can't tell a child too often that you love them, and that goes double for the healthy ones.

We were delighted when, in June, Erin had the opportunity to shine in the spotlight. For the past seven years she had participated in a unique dance program called Dance The Next Generation, or DNG. It is a youth scholarship program affiliated with The Sarasota Ballet. They recruit third and fourth graders to study dance with them, and in return for a seven-year commitment to the dance program, the dancers have the opportunity to earn a college scholarship. It's a wonderful program that includes lessons in classical ballet as well as jazz and modern dance. The students also have the opportunity to perform in the professional productions. For the past seven years we had watched Erin grow up performing with the company in The Nutcracker. By the time she was in high school she had danced almost every child part from party girl to soldier to dancing bon-bon.

Although she had tendon problems that limited her ability to dance on point and she never progressed to the higher levels that some of the more serious dancers did, she flourished socially and enjoyed the backstage friendships. To their credit, the ballet company never penalized her because she wasn't one of the stars. She was given instruction at her level and received a fair combination of love and discipline. Even though the program wasn't designed to create future prima ballerinas (its mission is to promote a love of the dance, and provide a character-building experience) it was much easier for the naturally gifted students to stick it out over the years. Most of the time the girls danced three times a week, and even more when they were in rehearsal. We told Erin many times how proud we were of her commitment and hard work.

In June of 1999 Erin had completed her seven-year requirement and was eligible to graduate from the program and receive her scholarship. Besides her dance commitments she had been required to maintain at least a "B" average during her years of participation. Her final requirement was to make a speech before a packed house at The Sarasota Opera House. There had been forty dancers who had started the program with her class seven years before, and now only eight remained.

Erin had practiced her speech at home earlier. It was thoughtful and well written, but when she had read it to us she spoke so rapidly that we could barely understand her.

"Don't worry," she'd said when we had expressed our concern. "I'll do fine, you'll see."

And she was dazzling. Standing tall and beautiful, poised and articulate, our little girl had suddenly grown up. All of those years of performing had made her appear very relaxed and confident on stage. She spoke of the values she had learned and the friendships she had made over the years. She had blossomed into a beautiful young woman.

Her graduation from DNG gave us a much-needed opportunity to focus on her for a few days, rather than Chris. It's very easy for the healthy siblings to get lost in the shuffle, and it takes a conscious effort to remind them that they matter also. With Jarrod, a lunch at McDonald's and a romp on the playground was usually all it took to placate him, but a teenager needs parents who accept not only them, but their world as well. For Erin, the dance and her friends had been the center of her world. We were glad to be part of it.

At that time we also made the decision to allow Chris to repeat fifth grade the following year. He had said over and over, "I'm not ready for middle school." Once again I had that eerie feeling that maybe he knew something we didn't. Later, we would not regret that we had let him make that choice.

In July Chris had the opportunity to attend ROCK Camp again. He brought back photos of horseback riding, a hot air balloon ride, and counselors with green slime on their faces. But this year he told of us a special girl he'd danced with.

By now Chris was twelve and I had smiled, remembering my first crush at that age. I tried to imagine Chris dancing with a girl, their shy smiles and maybe a hesitant embrace. But they wouldn't have that awkward silence that so many young adolescents experienced—they were cancer survivors. They were dancing into adulthood as ones who had already suffered, dancers who had already experienced things that children shouldn't have to. I would imagine that that would make the whole camp experience even more meaningful.

"When I have a girl, she'll be my babe, and I'll take her everywhere." Chris had said when he got home. "I'll drive her out to the beach in my convertible, then we'll go out to eat."

I thought about what a wonderful boyfriend, husband, and father Chris would be. Some lucky girl would get a kind, funny, sensitive young man. I hoped. I hoped that Chris would attend many more dances. I prayed that Chris would stay in remission and have the chance to dance through life.

When the new school year began Chris continued to do well. He was tolerating his weekly shots and nightly pills, and his labs were good. I no longer thought of him as a cancer patient, but as a survivor. He didn't mind going back to Bay Haven and being with a different, younger group. As a matter of fact he enjoyed the fresh start with new friends who hadn't known him when he was bald and sick. And I must admit, I loved having him with me at school.

He still talked his dad into skipping school after the weekly clinic appointments and going out to lunch at The Old Salty Dog. They saw every new movie as soon as it was released. Bobby called it their "bonding" time. Sometimes the teacher in me would admonish them for playing hooky, but looking back on it, I'm so glad that they didn't listen to me.

On one of their weekly trips to the clinic Bobby and Chris learned that little Jasmine had died. Jasmine was Tony and Diana's little girl. The last that we heard from them Jasmine had completed all of her treatments and was doing well. We were shocked. She had been 2 Southwest's little doll-baby, always dressed in pretty little outfits and matching headbands. She had been calm and cheerful and hardly ever got sick from the chemo.

By the time we found out, Jasmine had been gone for months. Bobby invited Tony to a Bucs game, and I asked Diana and her other two children if they'd like to come for a visit while the guys were at the game. She spent the afternoon with me and told me the story of Jasmine's passing. Jasmine had indeed successfully completed her treatment, but in a cruel twist of fate, she had died from an infection. Diana related how quickly the infection took over her little body. There was nothing they could do. As she was speaking I recalled how Jasmine had had a lot of hospitalizations for port infections. Diana believed that her immune system never fully recovered from the treatments.

But it was Diana's other beliefs that amazed me. She was calm, almost serene, when she spoke of her little angel. "I think Jasmine was going to relapse, so God sent that infection so she wouldn't have to suffer any more," she explained. Diana was completely at peace with Jasmine's passing. She even showed me photographs of Jasmine laying at rest in her coffin. Jasmine wore a silky white dress and looked like a sleeping angel.

Maybe some people would think that passing around photos of your dead child is a bit morbid, but it seemed to provide comfort to Diana. She wasn't mourning the loss of her little girl as much as she was celebrating her passage into Heaven. Diana exhibited a spiritual strength that I truly admired.

After spending a day with her I said my prayers of thanks for having Chris with us, and I couldn't help but wonder that if we lost Chris I'd be as accepting as she. That visit just steeled our resolve to make every day count. With the holidays approaching, we decided to surround ourselves with family.

Christmas that year was the best Christmas I'd ever had, and probably ever will have. We went up to the Pocono Mountains in Pennsylvania, where my parents have a house. While we were up there each of my three siblings came up with their families to visit and ski and eat, and just be together.

By day we'd head out to the ski slopes and the kids would take a morning lesson while the adults did their hard skiing. Jarrod wanted to snowboard like his big brother, so when we signed him up for lessons he ended up in a very small class since most of the other six-year-olds were in the ski classes. In the afternoon we all hit the slopes together. Jarrod was proud to be boarding alongside Chris.

In the evening we partied. I had quality time with my two brothers, Pat and Tim, and my sister, Maureen. Among the four of us we live in four different states, so our time all together is rare. Bobby has most of his family in Florida, so he graciously agreed to spend the holidays with my side.

It was the kind of Christmas you could put on a greeting card—family, snow, and a warm fire in the evening. And that week Chris finished his protocol. Sometime between Christmas and New Years Chris took his final pill. He held up the last 6 MP and we all toasted him with our wine glasses. I remember thinking that the pills had probably been unnecessary for quite some time since Chris had now been in remission for over two years. I have never been more wrong.

Chris, Jarrod, and Erin posing for a Christmas photo in 1994

Chris (foreground) in the hospital playroom during his first protocol

Chris playing with hospital friends on a good day

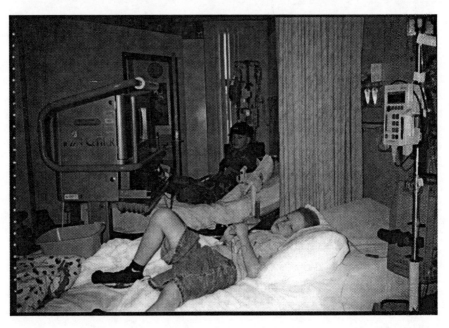

The side effects of the chemo often made Chris nauseous

Maribeth and Chris at a fund-raising event for The Leukemia and Lymphoma Society (formerly The Leukemia Society of America)

Chris's school photo from the fall of 1997

Chris visits with The Harlem Globetrotters

Chris was in his element snowboarding at Lake Tahoe

Chris speaks to the media at his bone marrow drive while the family looks on

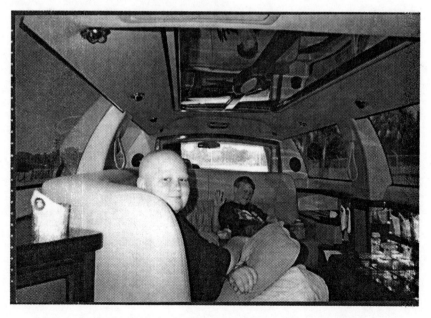

Chris and Jarrod chilling in the limo during Chris's shopping spree just a few months before his passing

Jarrod, Chris, and Erin in spring of 2001

Jose, Chris, and Erin on one of their last outings together

This family portrait was taken five days before Chris's passing. Chris knew that it was the last picture that would ever be taken of him, yet he smiled in every pose.

PART III

CHRIS'S SECOND PROTOCOL: 2000–2001

9

RELAPSE

With the arrival of the New Year and the new millennium we were full of hope and looking forward to better times ahead. Once again we felt like we had a future—a future full of delightfully normal family activities. Chris was finished with his weekly shots, and for the first time since his diagnosis he was only required to report to the clinic on a monthly basis. The visits would involve only blood work, no shots or painful procedures. January would be his first month off, and his last.

In January Chris decided to use his magic kit to prepare a show for Jarrod's kindergarten class. He would retreat to his room and practice, and when he was satisfied that he had mastered enough tricks to fill a performance he'd test his tricks on us. Jarrod begged him to explain his secrets, but Chris would say, "Ah, I can't spoil the magic!" We scheduled his show during my planning time so that I could come down from my classroom and watch.

"Maybe you'll be the next David Copperfield," I said.

It was wonderful that now Chris's biggest worry was performing for a bunch of five-year-olds!

But it was a brutally brief trouble-free honeymoon, for soon we had something new to worry us.

In late January Chris had come into our bedroom one morning. "Mom and Dad, one of my balls looks bigger than the other."

"Well, one of mine's a little bigger too, it's probably nothing," Bob had responded, "but let me take a look."

There was a size difference, Bob had reported, but it didn't look significant. We decided not to panic, but we were glad that Chris had an upcoming clinic appointment. It was scheduled for February fourth, the same day as Chris's magic show. "Be sure you have him back in time for his show," I'd said.

But Chris never got the chance to perform.

Bobby called me at school just before 11:00 AM (about the same time Chris would have been arriving to do his magic show). "They think his enlarged testicle is cancer. It's bigger than when I looked at it last time. They want to take him into surgery right away."

The phone shook in my hand as the tears streamed down my face. My thoughts raced. The monster was back. "I'll be there as soon as possible."

I scrambled through the arrangements for Jarrod's care and the coverage of my class, and shortly found myself once again on the interstate on my way to St. Petersburg. Guilt followed my van like a shadow. "You should have taken him to the clinic the same day he noticed his enlarged testicle," it admonished, making my tears sting and my chest ache.

I don't remember where, but I grabbed a fresh notebook to start a new hospital journal.

February 4, 2000

… After waiting what seemed like forever Chris went into surgery and had his left testicle removed. Dr. Reisman did the surgery. The frozen biopsy confirmed leukemia. We are to call Monday for more details. In about a week we will get full pathology results and the oncology staff will decide on a course of treatment.

While Chris was waiting for surgery I went over to the clinic to talk to the doctors. It was like a dream, a bad dream. Nothing is definite yet, but most likely Chris will have to get his port back in and endure more chemotherapy. Just when we thought life was going back to normal.

Questions:

1. Do you think the cancer was there all along? Ans: Probably.

2. Will you biopsy the other testicle? Ans: Yes.

3. Will Chris need radiation? Will he be sterile? Ans: Most likely to both.

4. Will you do another bone marrow aspiration (the test to see if there is leukemia in the marrow)? Ans: Yes.

5. If you find leukemia in the bone marrow aspiration does that mean that he has also relapsed in his bone marrow? Ans: Yes.

The surgery went well, as well as can be expected for the partial castration of my son. Later, while Chris was in recovery I went up to 2 Southwest—how strange and scary to realize that we shall once again become frequent visitors. When I got off the elevator on the second floor it seemed like they all already knew. News spreads fast. The clinic staff had suggested that I speak with Nurse Nancy, our "Smelly Melly." Apparently she has taken care of several testicular relapse patients.

She was very encouraging, stating that all of the boys that she had known with testicular relapse had survived and done well. She promised to hook us up with a survivor when Chris was ready …

Back downstairs in short stay/surgery Chris wanted to go home the minute he woke up, but it took a while. He threw up several times before he could keep anything down. He told us that he wished he were at school. Poor guy, he just wants to be a regular kid again. My heart is breaking.

After Chris recovered we were able to take him home for the weekend. The doctors needed time to look at his test results and figure out what to do with him. For us it was a weekend of agony. We all had to come to grips with the fact that Chris's hard-fought remission had been snatched away. We also knew that relapse meant that his chances for survival had dropped drastically.

Once again, Bobby and I found ourselves in the precarious position of being honest with Chris while trying to remain hopeful and upbeat. He was two years older now, and had a lot more questions than he did the first time around. We encouraged him to ask questions at the hospital as well.

When Chris returned to his room he was pensive. I saw the forgotten magic kit lying in a corner. Tears welled up in my eyes when I thought of the show that never was. Chris should be standing in front of a captive group of kindergarteners swooshing his cape and waving his wand. Instead, he stood in front of months of terrifying uncertainty. How I wished that his magic could make the cancer disappear.

February 8, 2001

Chris was admitted today to begin his new protocol. First we went to the clinic for the bone marrow aspiration. Dr. Rossbach did the procedure with Nurse Adam (Spike) assisting …

I'll always remember it as "high noon." It was about 12:00 noon as we waited anxiously for the results—Adam obligingly flapping the slides (containing Chris's marrow samples) in the air so that they would dry more quickly. My heart raced as I saw Dr. Rossbach walk briskly past us down the hall. Where was he going?

Seeing me hovering in the hall, Dr. Grana approached. "The results were questionable," she said, "so Dr. Rossbach went to pathology to get a better look. They have a better microscope."

I knew what that meant. They had found something. We were about to live our worst nightmare. Bobby and I paced. Chris sat in the treatment room and watched a "Star Wars" movie. We paced some more. Finally Dr. Rossbach came back and said that there were a few blasts in his bone marrow. "Early infiltration" he called it.

The day had a dream-like quality with stabs of painful reality.

Questions:

1. Are you going ahead with the radiation to his testicles? Ans: Yes.

2. Will he be sterile? Ans: Yes.

3. Are you going to do a bone marrow transplant? Ans: Probably not. Lack of a sibling match makes transplant very risky. We feel more chemotherapy is a better option.

4. What will the new protocol be like? Ans: It's called Cogum, and it's a year of inpatient followed by a year of outpatient.

5. Will the chemo be harder than the first protocol? Ans: Yes.

6. Dr. Rossbach, if it were your son would you do the chemo instead of the transplant? Ans: Yes.

We were relieved that the doctors weren't recommending transplant, but the new protocol sounded awful. Instead of seven months in and out of the hospital, this time it would be twelve. It seemed to stretch before us like a prison sentence.

We kept reassuring Chris that the Cogum protocol worked. We told him what the nurses had said about knowing several survivors. We didn't dwell on the fact that his relapse had significantly reduced his chances for survival.

When we questioned the doctors further about transplant versus chemotherapy, and they explained that in Chris's situation the survival rate for the two treatments was about the same, but with bone marrow transplant the risk factors were greater. A bone marrow transplant involves complete destruction of the immune system with powerful drugs and full body radiation. This puts the patient at great risk for life-threatening infection. Had they chosen transplant for Chris he would have to be given marrow from an unrelated donor since no one in our family matched. This would present a significant chance of a potentially life-threatening condition known as graft versus host disease—when the body identifies the donated marrow as foreign and rejects it. If the body launched a severe attack on the new bone marrow, the patient could die a miserable death.

Chris also seemed greatly relieved that he wasn't facing transplant. We had seen several children die during that process. He was, however, concerned about the testicular radiation. He took our advice and questioned Dr. Grana about it. "Does that mean I can never have any kids?" he asked.

"Well, there's more than one way to have children," Dr. Grana replied. You can adopt. But, no, chances are you won't be able to produce enough sperm to make children yourself."

"Will I have to go through the rest of my life with just one ball?"

"You don't have to, Chris. When you're older you can get a prosthetic so no one will be able to tell."

"Will I still be able to have a girlfriend and get married?"

"Yes, you'll be able to function like a normal healthy adult, and do all the things other males do."

Later, Bobby clarified this further. "You'll still be able to get hard-ons, buddy, you'll just be shooting blanks."

"But don't you be using that as an excuse to have dozens of girlfriends," I added, trying to lighten the mood.

But Chris ignored my lame joke and remained serious and thoughtful, "I'll never have kids of my own. They'll never have my freckles and sense of humor."

"You know there's lots of orphans in the world who need a good home. You'll make some lucky children a wonderful father," I said.

I was so proud of how he had handled things. In the space of a few days he had learned that his cancer had returned, he'd faced surgery, and been told he would never have children of his own. Instead of panicking he'd asked mature, thoughtful questions. He was dealing with all of this at the age of twelve, when most young boys are just beginning to discover their sexuality. Chris had to come to grips with losing a part of his before he even experienced it.

And what a wonderful father he would be. I ached thinking that his genetic material wouldn't be passed on, but that was a small price to pay for saving his life.

February 8, 2000 (continued)

... How strange to be back up on 2 Southwest, and back at RMH. It's sad, terrifying, yet heartwarming, to see all of the concerned, familiar faces. I'm seeing old friends for all of the wrong reasons. Chris's nurse is Smelly Melly, and when we arrived we immediately started picking on her. The joking around bothered Bobby, and he decided to head home for some time alone. We deal with stress differently.

... I just can't believe we are here again. No one saw it coming. I had no longer even thought of Chris as a leukemia patient. I had promoted him to the category of "survivor," even thinking that his last doses of chemo were unnecessary formalities. How wrong I was. Those meds had been keeping the mighty beast at bay.

Tessa came over and went over Chris's new protocol. New drugs: VP-16, Etoposide, Ifosfamide, mesna, decadron, 6TG. He would also be getting some of the same drugs as before, such as the methotrexate. She rattled off more endless lists of side effects. I took notes like a student studying for a life and death test. Chris also had an echocardiogram and a chest x-ray. And tomorrow Chris will face more surgery. He gets a mediport put back in.

That night Chris couldn't sleep so I stayed in the room with him. So, after a sleepless night Chris headed back down to surgery. He was actually relieved to go because he couldn't wait to get rid of the IV in his arm. The mediport eliminates the need for it. While we were down in surgical holding I met Nurse Mati who would become a very good friend.

Like Bob and me, Mati was involved in distance running for Team in Training and she was currently training for a triathlon. Mati was a tiny, spitfire Spaniard with enthusiasm in her voice and love in her eyes. We became instant friends and made plans to run together. I was excited to have a buddy to run with while at the hospital.

Later in the day Chris started his chemo. Things seemed to be proceeding as planned until Dr. Barbosa spoke to me.

February 9, 2000

... Dr. Barbosa told me today that Chris might end up having a bone marrow transplant after all. How terrifying. It seems the final decision will come sometime after Friday when they get the results of his cytogenetic test. That is the test that analyzes cells and chromosomes from his bone marrow ... They may do a stem cell transplant ... Dr. B said that after he has all of the test results he would confer with other colleagues and clinics around the country ...

Dr. Cotter, the radiation doctor, stopped by to inform us about Chris's radiation treatments. He will receive ten treatments of radiation on his remaining right testicle. Dr. Cotter said that between the radiation and the chemo, Chris will most likely be sterile. Well, we already knew that.

... Chris is very down today. So am I ...

We had thought the chemo versus transplant matter was settled. Life's challenges always seem more surmountable when there is a clear plan. Now suddenly we didn't have that anymore. Apparently all of the doctors didn't agree on what to do with Chris. This was both confusing and frightening. While we were comforted by the fact that they were checking with experts around the country, we were alarmed by their uncertainty.

I pictured all of the oncologists sitting around a conference table arguing. Maybe they had a spinner that read, "transplant" on one side and "lotsa chemo" on the other. Perhaps they each took a turn spinning to see which side it landed on the most. I pictured hidden labels underneath each side of the spinner, one said "life" and the other "death." But we weren't allowed to peek.

February 10, 2000

Chris slept well last night, which meant I could sleep as well … We went up to the rooftop playground and saw Hudson, the trick therapy dog … They had scheduled IT MTX (methotrexate injected into the spine) until I reminded them that the MTX caused the white brain matter changes in Chris last time. So they delayed it and decided to do an MRI of his brain.

Afterward, Chris's friend Richard and his mom came up for a visit. This was great therapy for Chris. They played Nintendo, watched a movie, and played the video bingo together. When they hung Chris's chemo he hardly noticed.

The bingo was definitely the highlight of the evening. Chris was quite the little prankster. He called several times, changing his voice, pretending he was a crying five-year-old who didn't win, trying to order pizza, speaking in his "ET" voice, and pretending he was from a Chinese restaurant saying "your one thousand egg rolls are here!" We had a lot of laughs.

After Richard left Chris broke down and cried. He wanted so badly to return with him and be a regular kid.

My careful note taking had paid off. I had remembered something the current staff was unaware of. It had been more than a year since Chris had been given MTX in his spinals due to the brain damage it had caused. It wasn't surprising that they missed this considering the volume of cancer patients treated there, but it reaffirmed my resolve to stay vigilant and aware, and to keep asking lots of questions.

The MRI was the same as last time, which meant no new damage. Due to Chris's history, however, they changed his protocol to IT ARA-C rather than the MTX.

During that admission Chris had several more visitors, which helped to bolster his spirits. Richard came back again and stayed overnight at RMH. That enabled him to hang out with Chris a little later. Quite often Chris was most alert and felt the best in the evening. He was also able to chat with Paul on the phone.

Another advantage of having friends from school visit was the fact that they weren't likely to die anytime soon. After losing three friends during his first protocol Chris was wary of becoming close to other patients, and who could blame him? I suppose it's the same reason the doctors keep a professional distance. Anyway, friends from home were a much safer bet than risking the loss of another cancer buddy.

The disadvantage of relying on outside visitors (especially children) is that most have little or no understanding of what a cancer patient goes through. They don't understand why Chris is so exhausted and can't leap out of bed and play. They have school and other friends and sports to fill their day, while Chris's days often loom empty except for meds and limited activities. It was a small handful of compassionate families that bothered to make the two-hour round trip to spend time with Chris. At least with patient friends, they are already there, and they understand the pain.

That pain included dealing with the side effects of the new drugs.

February 12, 2000

Just before they were ready to hang Chris's VP16, his blood pressure became quite high. They tried to bring it down with ativan, an antianxiety medication, but that didn't work. Next, they tried procardia which did work ... Another change in his protocol: He is to get hydrocortisone with his VP16 because he reported some shortness of breath from his last dose. Hydrocortisone prevents reactions ... The nurses also give him a drug called mesna. This is given after the ifosfamide (Ifos for short), a strong chemo drug which is known to cause bleeding in the bladder. The mesna prevents this ...

The list of drugs Chris was on read like a pharmacological shopping list. I made sure that I wrote them all down and listed any observed side effects. Sometimes there was more than one drug to choose from when treating certain side effects. For example—zofran, benadryl, marinol, and ativan, were all drugs that could be used for nausea. Zofran was an IV drug given automatically with most chemo, but Chris could ask for something else if the zofran wasn't doing the trick. After trying several drugs Chris decided that he liked the ativan best. It made him feel better without making him too groggy. Interestingly, other parents reported quite different reactions in their children.

By the fourteenth, Chris was ready to go home for ten days. We still hadn't heard the results of the cytogenetic test or the final decision about transplant. Now we had to look forward to watching his counts drop, wondering if the new drugs would be harder than the old ones.

10

AN UNCERTAIN FUTURE

Chris managed to stay home for his scheduled ten days without major side effects, but as usual, he was wiped out from the chemo. Unfortunately, the time at home was anything but uneventful. Our beloved lab, Moonshine, was now eleven years old and suffering from hip problems and arthritis. His pills were no longer keeping him pain-free, and we could hear his pitiful whining all night long. In the morning he could barely get up. We had to make the difficult decision to put him down.

I'll never forget that day, and Chris's amazing spirit.

"Do you want to come?" I'd asked him.

"Of course, Mom," Chris had responded, surprised that I'd even had to ask.

It took two of us to hoist Moonshine's ninety pounds into my van. Moonshine lay on a towel in the back and Chris caressed him gingerly. "It's OK, boy, you're going to doggie Heaven. You'll be able to run again. There's fire hydrants every ten feet, bowls full of steak, and cute bitches everywhere."

Just to be sure, I asked the vet if he thought we were doing the right thing. He affirmed our decision then explained that Moonshine would simply get a shot and go peacefully to sleep. He gave us the option of being there and holding him.

"Oh, I don't know if I want to watch," I'd said.

"Mom!" Chris admonished. "We have to be there for him."

So there was my son, teaching the teacher a lesson. The two of us hugged Moonshine with tears in our eyes as he took his last gentle breath. I closed my eyes and remembered the day we had brought Moonshine home as a six-pound puppy. Chris had been a tow-headed toddler scrambling after him, laughing at the deadly tail that thumped anything in its path. Now Chris, who had just been presented with his own uncertain future, was tenderly guiding his dog toward that fate that awaits us all.

Wasting no time, Bob brought home another dog—a Jack Russell Terrier that he'd heard about on the radio. The elderly owner could no longer keep her. Her name was Tobi and she was pretty much the exact opposite of Moonshine. Instead of large and lumbering we now had small and hyper. She couldn't take the place of Moonshine, but she was amusing nonetheless. "I wish I had some of her energy," Chris remarked.

On the day that he was scheduled to begin his next round of chemo Chris spiked a high fever.

February 23, 2000

Bobby brought Chris in to start his chemo, but they were unable to do so due to fever. Chris's temperature went up to 103 degrees. They had to take a culture and they'll watch it for twenty-four hours. They won't start chemo until he's been fever-free for at least twenty-four hours. Bobby reported that Chris was achy, tired, and not feeling well. They put him on IV antibiotics ...

With Chris feeling so miserable it was a relief that they couldn't start the chemo. Secretly I was hoping that the antibiotics would make him feel better, but that the fever would linger a little longer so he could get more of a break.

February 24, 2000

I came up around 11:00 AM and Bobby left. Chris started to perk up a little bit. We visited with Bryce (a lung cancer patient) and his mom, Belinda. Chris did a few magic tricks, but the best trick was the one he played on Nurse Dawn. Chris hid a can of green Silly String under his covers then called Nurse Dawn in. He told her that he was sneezing and had a lot of mucus. He then hid the can behind his hand as he let out a giant "Achooo" and sent green Silly String snotting through the air. Poor Dawn almost had to be resuscitated. As a matter of fact, I think Chris offered to do a mouth to mouth ...

During this hospital admission Chris lost his hair again. We knew it was inevitable, but it's still a shock when it happens. Like last time, Chris began shedding all over like a dog, but unlike last time, Chris decided to have some fun with it.

February 24, 2000 (continued)

... Grandmommy and Grandad came up to visit today. They went into the parent/ conference room down the hall and played checkers. When Chris got jumped by Grandmommy he said "Oh darn!" and yanked out an enormous clump of hair. Poor Grandmommy tried not to gasp, but couldn't help herself ... Later, while I was sitting

by Chris's bedside reading he reached over and placed several locks of hair on the page. "Bookmarks," he stated ...

Once again, Chris's irrepressible humor had triumphed over a potentially traumatic situation. By the end of the day his hair was falling out so fast that it was impossible to keep his pillow and bed clear, but we couldn't talk him into shaving and getting it over with. It had to be on his terms. Finally, it was another patient who gave him the solution.

February 25, 2000

... More wads of hair everywhere. Clump city. Everyone is offering to give Chris a hair cut, but he's refusing ... Finally Bryce stopped by and told Chris how he just plucked all of his hair out into a bowl. Chris liked that idea, so I fetched him a yellow tub and he plucked away. He filled the entire bucket, and when he was done he was completely bald ...

By the following day, which was a Saturday, Chris had been fever-free for twenty-four hours so they started his chemo. This part of his cycle called for large doses of IV MTX, thirty-six hours worth. Although they had discontinued the IT MTX (in the spine), Chris would continue to receive the drug both intravenously, and also as leg shots. We knew from experience that he would probably feel well for a day, then start to get sick after the first twenty-four hours. As expected, Chris felt sick on Sunday and he asked me to stay in the room with him that night. So I pulled out a comfortable blue recliner that converted into an uncomfortable bed, and kept him company. Even though I knew that I had to go back to work on Monday, my most important job was being there for Chris.

February 28, 2000

I didn't get much sleep last night, but Chris finally seems to be resting comfortably. He finished his last bag of MTX. I left at 7:45 AM and went back to Sarasota to work. Bobby came up an hour or so after I left.

Later, I spoke with Chris by phone and he sounded great. He told me that his teacher at Bay Haven, Jane Keil, had the entire class speak to him on the phone. One by one they had lined up at her desk to take a turn saying "hi." Chris had really enjoyed it.

Since Chris's relapse I had resumed my three-day work schedule. It was very hard leaving Chris when he was in the hospital. Even though I knew Bobby was there, I still felt guilty and misplaced—like I wasn't where I was supposed to be.

But I kept telling myself that Erin and Jarrod needed me, too. I wanted to be able to take Jarrod to baseball and Erin to ballet. And I knew that Bobby cherished his time alone with Chris. Still, a part of me envied the hospital moms who didn't work and could be by their child's side constantly.

Chris came home on Tuesday, but the high doses of methotrexate took their toll. In less than a week he was back in the hospital for mucusitis (the awful mouth sores) and bone pain. He couldn't eat or sleep. As if that weren't bad enough, we had another animal tragedy in the family while Chris was in the hospital.

March 6, 2000

Chris was admitted today for pain control, fluids, and nutrition. They also put him on antibiotics—the same two, I think, that he was on last week ... Chris is on a morphine pump for the pain, and he's also on oxygen because the morphine tends to make breathing shallow ...

Bob called and told me that Tobi killed Kiwi (Chris's parrot). Kiwi got out of his cage and was no match for the pouncing terrier. No one was home when it happened. First we lost Moonshine, and now Chris's beloved bird. How in the world are we going to tell him?

The next several days could only be described as miserable. Chris's sores had gone all the way down his esophagus and into his intestinal tract. He even had sores around his anus, which made it painful to go to the bathroom. We decided to put off telling him about Kiwi. Finally, by Thursday the ninth, he felt better.

Whenever I wasn't up at the hospital I told Bob to keep the journal updated. His entries were usually short and clinical like a medical chart. He would record Chris's meds, his activity level, whether or not he was eating, and not much else. But this time Bob poured his heart out.

March 9, 2000 (Bob's entry)

... I'm sitting here looking at my son. He's somewhat sleeping, all these gadgets hooked up to him, Hyper-Al, lipids, (the IV nutrition), antibiotics, narcan to help him urinate (difficulty urinating is a side effect of morphine), morphine, oxygen ... his hair gone and his skin pale. I have to think positive or I'll get emotional. I've already cried a lot. Why can't he be playing with his friends? I've prepared myself emotionally for the worst, at least I think I have ... I pray many times a day that the worst won't happen, but I still have to think of it. I don't dare tell other people about it; they wouldn't understand and they'd probably think I was morbid. But they don't know what it's like to have a child in this situation.

When Chris relapsed on February fourth it was the same time Jarrod was starting his T-ball. My first thought was that Jarrod wouldn't be able to play, but then I thought more about it and said, "No way." I'm a parent of three kids—not just one. Jarrod has a life too. I had to get him to baseball. No, I mean "we." Maribeth and I are a great team. Thank God I have her. I wouldn't be able to get through this without her. She's a very strong person.

It's not like me to sit here and put my feelings on paper, but I'm so glad I did. It's some release. Every little bit helps.

Reading Bobby's entry reminded me how lucky I was to have him for a husband. As he had said, we were a good team. The tremendous strain of Chris's cancer had brought us closer together rather than driven us apart.

I also thought about how therapeutic journaling had been for me, and I was glad that Bob could participate. I think all families struggling with serious illness would benefit from the practice.

Chris made it home the following day, but was only given a five-day hiatus. He had to report back on the sixteenth for more chemo, and also for a bone marrow aspiration to see if he was back in remission.

Chris accepted the news of Kiwi's demise in the same manner that he had endured all of his other challenges. At first, he was tearful and devastated, but then he became philosophical, and added Kiwi to his list of Heavenly creatures.

Eventually, we had to give up on Tobi, who never settled down, and became quite destructive. We gave her to a shelter that assured us that she would be adopted and not destroyed. That paved the way for the addition of two new fuzzy family members—a brother and sister pair of pugs that Chris named "Gizmo" and "Bugsy." They possessed the sweet temperament of our lab, Moonshine, but they were small enough to pick up and cuddle. They would become a great comfort to Chris and to all of us.

March 16, 2000

Today Chris finally had his bone marrow aspiration, and it was clean! He's back in remission. Now we'll pray every day that he'll stay that way!

Chris's bed wasn't ready so we went out to lunch and had a great time ...

... Cleared for chemo later in the evening. (They test ph level of urine.) I reminded them that Chris is supposed to get a reduced dosage of his vincristine due to his terrible back pain last time ... Tonight Chris starred once again in the video bingo game. He rolled the ball with the numbers in it and called them out in his now famous "ET" voice. It was fun sitting in the background egging him on ...

The clean bone marrow aspiration was the best news in the world. It meant that the drugs were working. It was a huge hurdle that we had overcome. Now the long months of treatment ahead seemed a little more bearable. Also, when Chris was really down or miserable we could reassure him. "The treatment's working. You're in remission."

Also, I enjoyed the days when I could be with Chris in the beginning of his admissions because he still felt well. I could follow him around from one activity to the next and be his assistant prankster.

... At crafts Chris made a plaster cast of his hand, and painted it bright colors. He attached it to the pump on his IV pole. It looked quite attractive ...

... Chris went up to the nurses' station, and found the intercom button for Mitchell Dodson's room (Mitchell is a teenage leukemia patient). Chris pushed it and very loudly sang "The Barney Song" (a syrupy song from a preschool TV show). So much for Mitchell's nap ...

The following day was a good one as well. It was St. Patrick's Day, and I decided that it was my duty to paint shamrocks on everyone's faces. By noon all of the nurses and several patients had shamrocks on their cheeks. Of course Chris had to be different. He had me paint a giant yellow smiley face on top of his bald head, and jagged green stitches down the side of his face.

Chris had a visit from one of his teachers and her daughter. They brought an enormous plastic tub full of toys and activities. A high school club as a community service project had adopted Chris! His teacher, Kathy Fenton, had known how much Chris loved putting together Star Wars Legos, so the bin was packed with them. What a wonderful gift!

Bobby came up later in the day and asked Chris if he wanted anything from the store. Chris mentioned a few items then added, "Don't forget my hair gel." We laughed all the way out to the car.

The rest of that hospital admission was bearable. Chris required medicine to control his blood pressure, but he fared much better than last time. However, there were a few problems on the home front.

On the night that Bobby and I were both at the hospital with Chris we had allowed Erin, who was now seventeen, to stay home alone. That resulted in a huge party. Bobby had gone home to find beer bottles blossoming in the bushes. "But, Dad," Erin had explained, "I couldn't help it. The doorbell kept ringing, and people just kept walking in." She had made it sound like an act of nature.

After much lecturing from us Erin asked us how long she was grounded for. "Oh, you're not grounded," we responded. "You're just going to be spending a lot more time with us and Chris. From now on you're staying with us at The Ronald McDonald House when we're both up there."

"Can't you just ground me?" Erin pleaded.

That was all part of our parental juggling act—tricky business with a chronically ill child. Erin was at an age when she craved independence, but wasn't ready to assume the responsibilities. So when we tried to draw her closer and include her in the hospital visits she sulked and behaved as if she were being subjected to medieval torture.

Jarrod, on the other hand, loved the hospital and the RMH. He enjoyed the novelty of new toys and the attention from the nurses and volunteers. But he was exhausting to be around. He couldn't sit still and was often seen zooming up and down the hallways in a wagon or stroller. He sometimes annoyed Chris who would ask him to leave the room when he was being particularly noisy, which was quite often. Most of the time it was easier for one of us to stay home with the other kids. But we couldn't help feeling torn, because we had such precious little time together as a family.

After that admission Chris was scheduled to stay home until April, but six days after his release he spiked a fever. He was miserable with mouth sores and back pain. They also found an abscess in his rectum. Even with his increased dosages of both his fluids and the rescue drug, leucovoran, poor Chris continued to suffer from nasty side effects and unscheduled hospitalizations. So Bobby and I resumed our back-and-forth routine.

In the meantime, I had once again run out of sick days so my pay was being docked. We had to adjust our budget accordingly. Once again—that other cancer side effect—less income, more bills. Even with insurance our co pays for Chris's admissions, clinic visits, and prescriptions were hundreds of dollars a month. But I still counted my blessings.

Bobby had always been a hustler, and being self-employed he could seek out more work for extra income. I also never stopped appreciating the fact that there were two of us to share the burden. I had seen several single moms literally camping in their child's hospital room. They sat by their child's bed for days without a break, sometimes they had other children crammed in the room with them, babies in strollers, toddlers playing on the floor. Often they had no budget to adjust. They depended upon the kindness of others. Lynda, the social worker, stayed busy finding many families' assistance just so their electricity wasn't cut off.

Bay Haven continued their blessings as well. Marilyn knew that I wouldn't ask her for financial help, so in her own delightfully sneaky way she held a fund-raiser behind my back. The staff and families collected over $3,000.00 and opened a special bank account for us. I was awestruck. "I can't take this," I said.

"Sorry, you have no choice," Marilyn beamed putting her arm around me. "You're just going to have to accept the fact that we love you."

And that's what it always came down to. Chris was coping with the support of our love. We were coping with the loving support of our family and our community. I felt like God was there among us. We couldn't begin to guess why our beautiful son had to suffer so much, but their was no doubt that many people were reaching out to help us.

By mid-April Chris's mental outlook was starting to deteriorate. He was crying more and more during his hospital admissions. He cried when visitors left; he cried for his dead parrot; he cried for his lost childhood. Some days there was no way to cheer him up. What do you say to someone who has every right to cry?

Finally, we consulted with the staff pediatric psychiatrist who put Chris on antidepressants. He informed us that many adolescents undergoing chemotherapy were taking antidepressants. In addition to the situation being very stressful many of the chemo drugs themselves had a depressant effect on the brain.

May was a better month. The antidepressants helped, and Chris was less weepy in the hospital. Chris didn't have any unscheduled admits either so he had more recovery time at home. That meant more precious time to be normal. He was able to attend his cousin's first communion and the party afterward. Activities that we once took for granted were now cherished moments in time.

We bought Chris a battery-powered scooter. It went about fifteen miles per hour, and he loved it! Being unable to walk far or ride his bike, the scooter gave Chris freedom to zip around the neighborhood. It put him back in contact with friends he hadn't seen in a while so it was wonderful therapy.

Chris was able to attend school a little bit that month as well. We were so proud of the courage he showed walking in the halls to class, waving, smiling, with no hat covering his bald head.

He also showed a lot of courage when his radiation treatments began.

May 4, 2000

... *What a strange, sad feeling watching my son being sterilized. First they laid him down on a narrow table and they used small laser beams to pinpoint the exact spots they would radiate (his scrotum and the remaining right testicle). Then they asked me to leave the room for the actual procedure, which was painless. I was able to watch on camera from just outside as they positioned the apparatus, which looked like a typical x-ray machine. It took only a minute. I couldn't stop thinking about what Chris had said earlier, "I'll never have kids with my freckles and sense of humor."* ...

The side effects of the radiation were minor compared to the chemotherapy—just some redness and itching not unlike a sunburn. It didn't stop Chris from his antics. One time he brought his monkey puppet "Squeaky." Squeaky seemed to tolerate the treatments quite well also. One day at the clinic when Dr. Rossbach saw the puppet he disappeared into a back room for a moment then emerged with a monkey puppet of his own! It seemed that the doctor had been consulting with his own puppet assistant, "Herman the German."

Chris also amused himself with my laptop computer. After his relapse Bay Haven had given me the laptop to use for as long as I needed it. It was a godsend. I could e-mail lesson plans to Laurie, and use it to enter grades and do report cards. It enabled me to be in constant communication with the school which sent out almost all of its memos electronically. But Chris found other, more creative uses for it.

May 26, 2000

... Chris has discovered that some of the games on the computer allow the user to name a file then have the computer say the name out loud. It has a very sexy female voice, so Chris has taken to naming his files, "Chris, will you go out with me?" Depending upon who happened to be in the room the computer has also been known to blurt out such things as, "Chemo sucks," "Butthole," "Eat corn," "Chris rules," and others. I made him delete the inappropriate ones, but not before we had a good laugh. It was an excellent way to pick on Nurse Nancy. We have also been downloading and saving blonde jokes!

Having the laptop was good therapy for me as well. Through e-mail I renewed my long-distance friendship with my college roommate, Barb. We began e-mailing each other daily and she became my e-therapist. Like me, she had become a teacher and was raising a family as well. Bob and I had spent a lot of time with Barb and her husband, Dan, during our college days. We were close and I could vent my frustrations to her online.

When Barb found out that Chris and I were collecting blonde jokes she made it her mission to forward me as many as she could find. This meant that whenever Nurse Nancy was within earshot we had lots of ammunition to fire at her.

"Hey, Smelly Melly," Chris said one day, "What do you do when a blonde throws a grenade at you?"

"Look, you Ditmars people, I have work to do. I have to go take care of some of my *nice* patients."

"You pull out the pin and throw it back!"

The best part was watching her trying to hide her smile as she pretended to huff her way out of the room.

The first half of June we enjoyed a couple of quality weeks at home. The highlight was our special family limo ride. Chris's thirteenth birthday, Bobby's birthday, and our anniversary all fell within one week. We decided we'd celebrate them all at once by renting a limo for a few hours. We had learned to grab for the gusto when Chris's counts were up. Erin and Jarrod each invited one friend, and Chris had two buddies: his cousin Andrew, and his best friend, Paul.

Inside the limo had neon lights that continuously changed color. It was like being in the land of Oz. We cruised around town in style stopping at all the favorite places where Bobby and Chris often had their lunches. At Hooters the girls all kissed Chris and gave him a T-shirt with all of their signatures. At The Olde Salty Dog the manager brought out Chris's favorite clam chowder. In the middle of the cup floated a cracker with a candle on it. It was a fabulous day!

It wasn't long before we were back in the hospital having days that were somewhat less than fabulous. On the second day of his next chemo admit Chris woke up in extreme pain.

June 20, 2000

Chris woke up in so much pain this morning. The vincristine is really hurting his back and legs. He was writhing and crying with his teeth clenched. Nurse Paula got him a cotylenol, but that didn't help much. The doctors were all down the hall in the conference room, so we couldn't get more pain meds ordered until they were done. Finally, the nurse gave him some ativan and he fell asleep.

With the help of meds Chris slept a good portion of the day, which was probably a blessing. He had a few crying spells, but managed to cheer up for a little while when he was describing his birthday limo ride to Chaplin Peter.

He didn't want to get out of bed today, and turned down offers to participate in teen night activities. But he finally had to get up because he got some diarrhea ...

There is absolutely nothing worse than seeing your child in pain, not boo-boo I-scraped-my-knee pain, but gut-wrenching pain, unpredictable pain. You want to snatch it away from them and make it your own, and you cry because you can't.

Even though the rise and fall of Chris's counts came in fairly predictable cycles, his episodes of discomfort varied greatly. His level of comfort could change drastically in a matter of minutes. Pain management became a very important issue.

There were times when the staff took a wait and see attitude before increasing pain meds, and we had to assert ourselves and say, "Hey, this isn't working." For the most part the doctors and nurses were quick to respond, but sometimes when the floor was busy we had to be persistent to get their attention. And Chris wasn't the type to complain, so we were glad we could be there to do it for him.

To his credit, Chris rarely felt sorry for himself when he was pain-free. His pity parties usually only lasted about ten minutes, then he could be coaxed into doing something fun.

June 23, 2000

... Chris had a very good day today ... he cut out a bunch of animal pictures from a "Ranger Rick" magazine. He plans to make a collage for his room ... Pestered Smelly Melly for a while. We're running out of blonde jokes. We'll have to get some more ... Chris was quite the character manning the phones on the bingo game tonight. He did his impersonations, and when the winners called in he ended each call by saying, "Well, all-righty then!" But the funniest thing was when Chris tried to stuff the ballot box. Each time a child got "bingo" they were allowed to enter their name in a drawing for a large stuffed animal. Chris kept making extra copies of his name and trying to sneak them into the box. Of course he got caught, so he removed all of the slips but one. And guess what? He won anyway! "Well, all-righty then!"

It wasn't unusual for a good day to be followed by a miserable one. When I got out of bed each day I never knew what to expect. My morning jogs were a very important stress reliever for me. By now I was running regularly with my nurse friend, Mati, and I had also recruited another companion, Emily, the eighteen-year-old daughter of The Ronald McDonald House manager. Mati's great conversations and Emily's youthful energy gave me a real boost. Together we explored the beautiful St. Petersburg waterfront and watched the morning sun shimmer and dance around the sailboats. Afterward, my leg muscles would feel all warm and tingly, and armed with a cappuccino, I'd march upstairs to Chris's room.

Often on weekends Bobby and I could be together up at the hospital. Many times our parents helped with the other two kids so we could be alone. When Chris slept or was comfortable watching TV we would take time out together at the RMH or go out. That down time together kept us communicating, and it kept us from drifting apart.

I saw the detrimental effects of hospital life on other couples. Sometimes one spouse couldn't bear to see their child suffer, and left hospital duty to the other. Other times one spouse was the sole breadwinner while the other one stayed with the sick child, and the time apart took its toll. One mother confided in me that she had discovered her husband was cheating on her while she spent long hours in the hospital with her son.

But for every sad story there was an uplifting one. Many parents pulled together, and made the most of their limited quality time, sharing meals and activities together in their child's room, but also paying attention to each other's needs.

Bobby and I consciously planned time alone together each week, even if it was only an hour. "Let's see if Chris feels OK after dinner, then we'll sneak out for an hour," Bobby would say. Sometimes I felt guilty, but I knew he was right. "Leave Chris your cell phone, and he'll call if he needs us," Bobby would reassure me. That was our time to cry on each other's shoulders, our time to be friends instead of caretakers.

On our outings we often frequented a little sandwich grill on the downtown pier. It was often the same man who took our order and one day he asked if we lived nearby. We explained that our son was a cancer patient who was frequently hospitalized at the children's hospital in town. When he found that out, instead of pouring our wine in the typical little plastic wine cups, he used the large paper beer glasses. "There you go!"

So that became a regular get-away spot. "Let's go get a bucket of wine," Bob would say.

Of course there were times when we argued and snapped at each other, times when we could barely stand to be in the same room together, but we always knew that we could count on each other. That knowledge was a powerful antidote to despair.

With one fever admit and two chemo admits July was another busy, roller-coaster month. At least school had ended and I could focus completely on Chris. The days continued to alternate between tolerable with amusing distractions, to downright depressing and miserable.

There was an elderly gentleman volunteer who frequented the floor. His name was Frank, and he took a special liking to Chris since they shared an interest in magic tricks. One day when Chris was feeling pretty well, Frank spent a lot of time with him.

July 3, 2000

... Frank the volunteer magician stopped by. He and Chris had a long conversation about different magicians and their tricks. I noticed that Frank was sharing a lot of his secrets with Chris. Frank, who is a cancer survivor, also shared that his cancer has returned in his throat and lungs. I wondered if that was why he was revealing all of his secrets ...

Pain management continued to be a challenge. The pain was often from mouth sores or bone pain, both very common side effects from the drugs. Sometimes the pain drugs themselves had side effects that had to be dealt with. For example, morphine was known to cause headaches, slow respiration, and difficulty urinating. So the doctors didn't like to keep their patients on it for extended periods of time. It was a constant dance to find the right level of comfort with the minimum amount of side effects.

Bob and I had to deal with the pain management at home as well. We were required to give Chris injections of neupogen, the drug that helped Chris's white cells recover from the chemo. It stimulated his bone marrow to produce cells at an abnormally rapid rate. Sometimes this resulted in severe leg and back pain.

It was an awful feeling having to give your child shots that you knew were going to hurt. Sometimes I had tears in my eyes as I injected Chris. "Buddy, I sure wish I could take these shots for you."

"Yeah, I wish you could, too," Chris would reply.

I had acquired an impressive bag of tricks to try and keep Chris's spirits up, but sometimes the bag was empty when it was time to bolster my own spirits.

July 11, 2000

... Most of the time it seems like I'm so in control—checking meds, telling jokes, but sometimes I just lose it, and cry or get furious over some little thing. I wish I had something to smash right now. I want to hear something else besides my life shatter into itsy bitsy little pieces ... The other day I took a wrong turn going to the grocery store. I banged my fist so hard on the steering wheel I bruised my hand. I was crying so much that I had to pull over. It's hard living your life in fear. I don't want Chris's name on a wall plaque on 2 Southwest: "In Loving Memory of Christopher Ditmars." I try to

visualize him as a young man, returning to this place to help others, telling his story on
telethons ...

To combat my own depression I made up a mental game I called "It Could be
Worse If." The game was simple. I would just compile mental lists of worse situations. It usually went something like this: It could be worse if Chris had cancer
and we were living in a hut with a mud floor in a third-world country with no
modern hospital. It could be worse if Chris hadn't regained remission. It could be
worse if I were a single mom with no job and no loving support network. It could
be worse if Chris had relapsed in his brain, then he might slowly go mad and not
even be able to recognize us. It could be worse if we lived in a war zone and had
to cross miles of minefields, and dodge sniper bullets on the way to the clinic. It
could be worse if Chris were going through this while I was sitting in prison on
death row about to be executed for a crime that I didn't commit ... And so on.
Sometimes I created scenarios that were so far fetched and ridiculous that I had to
laugh in spite of myself. Other times nothing worked and I just had a good cry.

Another sure way to cheer myself up was to find someone else to help. I had
become adept at jumping through the insurance hoops to get them to pay for
treatments and consultations that were initially denied. I shared some of my
tricks with a few of the other parents.

July 12, 2000

... I helped Wesley's (bone marrow patient) mom today sort through her pile of bills.
We sat the dining room table at RMH and she showed me all of the items that her
insurance company was refusing to pay for. Since I have the same insurance company
I knew that almost all of the bills should have been covered. They were mostly mistakes
made by overworked, underpaid clerks who failed to recognize that the various bills
were all related to her son's cancer diagnosis. It was with extreme pleasure that I wrote
an appropriately irate letter on her behalf. Ahhh, that felt good ... The remaining
bills, which no one could make any sense out of, we distributed to the RMH gals and
we had a contest to see who could make the best paper airplane!

During Chris's first protocol the bills had been a stressor for me, but by the
second time around I had devised an ingenious system for dealing with them. I
set up my own dummy nonprofit organization and called it "The Ditmars Family
Survival Foundation." I immediately elected myself president and chief corre-
spondent. I then created my own form letter, which I saved on my computer. For
each bill we received I printed one of my letters and sent it right back to them

along with the bill. It very politely stated that they were all a bunch of morons and they were trying to bill me for procedures and consultations that had already been approved and routed properly through my primary physician.

At one point we were being erroneously billed almost daily. Finally, I sent a family photo so they knew that we were actually real people. And to my utter amazement someone from the company actually called and apologized! I encouraged other bill-laden parents to do the same. "If you have a bald photo of your child to send, that's even better," I suggested.

When nothing could cheer him up Chris would deal with his pain and depression by sleeping as much as possible. Not a bad strategy—at least he could run and play soccer in his dreams.

It was at the end of July, when I came across an old journal entry of mine that I realized how many of those dreams had been indefinitely postponed. Each of the rooms at RMH has a journal on the nightstand. They call it "The Book of Hope." Families are invited to write about themselves if they care to. The journals are full of heartwarming prayers and heartbreaking medical stories. Sometimes I would read them at night and try to picture the sick babies and struggling children whose stories unfolded inside. But one night I found myself reading about myself.

July 31, 2000

In room 35 at RMH I saw an old entry of mine in the journal. It was dated February 8, 1998. In it I wrote that Chris was in for his last inpatient chemo. Little did I know! My entry was so full of hope and anticipation for the future. It spoke of Chris returning to school and our family resuming a normal life. How ironic—it was almost exactly two years later to the day (February 4, 2000) that his relapse was discovered. I guess I should update that journal ...

It was three years now that we had been dealing with Chris's cancer. I realized that our youngest, Jarrod, probably couldn't even remember what a normal life was like. Sometimes I couldn't remember either.

But this was my life's assignment, and all I could do was my best—laugh a little, cry, fall down, then get up and do my best some more. While Chris was asleep I'd often walk over to the RMH and stand at the railing at the edge of the patio behind the house. The back of the house overlooked a park that sloped downward so that the tops of palm trees stretched their fronds up to the railing. You could hear the birds twittering and see squirrels leap in the branches just a few feet away. Lizards and beetles scrambled about, not sure where the park ended and the patio began. It was there, late at night, that I did my talking to God.

"Please, Lord, let my Chris stay in remission," I'd pray. "Let him grow up and share his wonderful talents with the world. He's so funny and compassionate. He'll be such a good father someday. Maybe he'll be a comedian and do all of his great impersonations for everyone. Maybe he'll be a child-life counselor in a hospital and help other kids who are suffering. He has so much to offer. This world just wouldn't be the same without him." I'd watch my tears fall and make tiny puddles on the wooden railing.

Sometimes it felt like God was whispering an answer deep inside my heart, and after praying I'd feel calmer and somehow protected. Something inside me felt sure that no matter what, I'd be OK. But would Chris be OK? Was he destined to remain upon this Earth?

11

LIVING IN THE MOMENT

August brought no unexpected admissions, just two five-day chemo admits. For us that was an easy month. Chris continued to struggle with back pain, and they did tests to rule out bone damage. Bobby and I had some stress-related squabbles and I wrote an entry in my journal about how married life sucks.

I caught up with Bryce's mom, Betty (Bryce was the lung cancer patient who had advised Chris on hair plucking). Bryce had just had a bone marrow transplant and had become extremely sick. He had spent a few days in ICU, but now he was doing much better. Listening to all that Bryce had been through made me terrified of bone marrow transplant. I prayed that Chris wouldn't have to face that.

It was encouraging to hear about kids who made a turn for the better. It automatically bolstered my hopes for Chris. Chris received a visit from a young man who had also relapsed and gone through the exact same protocol. He was healthy and doing well. We needed to hear those positive stories because death was always lurking nearby.

August 1, 2000

... While Chris was sleeping I spoke to the mom of an angel today. Her name is Sheila, and her daughter Karen died last October. She would have been thirteen on Sunday. I thought she looked familiar. Then, as we were talking I remembered her, Karen, and Chris having a water fight one time. They had chased each other down the hall, IV poles in tow, laughing and blasting away with water pistols.

Sheila was up on the floor dropping off invitations to a dedication in her daughter's honor. She has created a beautiful garden in her yard in Karen's memory. The photos showed a bench and a plaque with an arched trellis overhead. Roses and numerous other plants bloomed all around. What a wonderful tribute.

I wonder what it must feel like to come back to this place after your child has died ... I hope I never find out.

As the months of this second protocol wore on, Chris had grown more content to stay in bed and decline activities. While we couldn't blame him, this was a cause for concern for several reasons. First, it wasn't helpful to his morale. It was much easier to distract and entertain him if he was busy. Also, there were medical concerns. His muscles would stiffen after prolonged inactivity, and if his counts were low, lying down all day put him at greater risk for pneumonia. So getting him up and about once or twice a day became one of our goals.

Fortunately, we were able to appeal to his sense of humor. One great asset in this department was the "fart machine."

Since bathroom humor seems to run deep in our family, Chris came by it naturally. Thus Chris's remote control fart machine was a great source of entertainment for us. The machine was simply a battery-powered speaker with prerecorded flatulence noises that were controlled by a small remote. Both the speaker and the remote control were small enough to hide easily.

I remember one of those hospital days when Chris hadn't been out of bed for a while and I was trying hard to convince him to get up and walk around. Finally, he agreed to do so only if I would put the fart machine in my back pocket, with him at the controls. (Ah, the things we do for our children!) So off we went to have some fun in the elevator.

We got on and Chris stood innocently in the back of the elevator, one hand on his IV pole, the other hand discreetly covering the remote. As more people stepped onto the elevator he allowed them to stand between us. Then, just as it filled with folks shoulder to shoulder and the doors shut, he pressed the button. I tried not to laugh as the raspberry sounds blasted from my back pocket. Oh my, how polite people can be when they pretend not to hear! They seemed to be in quite a hurry to get off as the doors reopened!

After a while I grew bolder and would let out a sigh of relief or a nice "Ahh-hhh" after each blast. It was funniest when other children got onto the elevator. They would be unable to suppress their giggles and comments, "Mommy, did you hear that?"

"Shhhh, be quiet, honey." The poor parent would be just as embarrassed as if she were the perpetrator. Chris and I would tumble out into the hallway howling with laughter before hopping onto the next elevator.

But we finally met our match when riding along with this one particular woman. She was a neatly dressed, elderly lady, barely over five feet tall. The three of us were alone in the elevator so the fart sounds seemed to reverberate off of the walls. Chris had really let it rip, and just as the doors opened for her to get off she paused momentarily and gently laid her hand on my arm. "Well, my dear, I bet you feel so much better now."

August 3, 2000

... The best part, however, was when we took the fart machine up to the room where they broadcast the Thursday night video bingo. Chris convinced me to sit on camera, with the fart machine tucked away out of sight. Soon everyone was laughing and flapping their hands in the air saying "Pheeewww!" I looked straight into the camera and said, "Kids, whatever you do don't order the blue plate special...."

Those moments of madness were priceless. It was our way of snatching back a small portion of Chris's lost childhood. And it certainly helped me stay in touch with my own inner child. When I think back on all of the best times in my life they were usually silly little moments, and more often than not those moments were more child-like than adult. I considered it one of my primary missions to give Chris as many of those moments as possible.

There were many fine organizations that also realized the need for these kids to get out and have a little fun. Chris continued to receive invitations to attend camps and sporting events. Many times we turned them down because Chris just wasn't up to it, but at the end of August Chris and Bobby accepted an invitation from Fred McGriff and The Tampa Bay Devil Rays to fly to a game in Baltimore as special guests of the team. He and Bobby went with a group of oncology patients and they enjoyed a day meeting the players and being treated as VIPs. Also, the community-minded Tampa Bay Buccaneers sent players several times a year up to the hospital to visit the patients, and Chris was able to meet several players and have his pictures taken with them. All of those CPs (Cancer Perks) as I jokingly referred to them, didn't make up for Chris's lost health, but it meant a lot to us that so many people cared.

In September Chris didn't have any unscheduled hospital admissions, either. This gave us a little more time to focus on his school situation. He was now in middle school, and having to face a whole new situation. Just as he had at Bay Haven, Chris was assigned a home-bound tutor who would come to the house two days a week. Whenever medically possible we encouraged Chris to attend school.

Middle school is hard enough when you're healthy. We had contacted all of his teachers and his guidance counselor ahead of time so they knew all about his situation, but I could only imagine how intimidating it must have been for Chris.

At Bay Haven Chris had attained an almost hero status, but now in this strange new school, he was just hoping to avoid being an oddity. I'll never forget the first day he summoned the courage to get onto a bus full of strangers. The school had a no-hat rule so the first thing everyone noticed about Chris was his bald head.

I asked him how his first day went. "It was OK," Chris shrugged. "Everyone in my classes was real nice, but I didn't like going out in the hallways. I couldn't get my locker open, and some kids pointed at me and called me "cue-ball." I wish I didn't look like a bald freak."

"You don't look like a bald freak," I'd responded. "You're an incredibly brave, strong young man—a lot more mature than those kids. Just look the name callers right in the eye and say. 'My name's Chris.' If they keep bugging you, hold your head up high and keep walking. With your great personality you'll make real friends, and you'll know those other losers don't matter."

Inside I didn't feel as calm as I sounded. I wanted to storm over to the school, gather the whole student body in an assembly and lecture them all about the trauma my son has endured. I wanted to send them all home with research assignments on the effects of cancer. When one particular tormenter persisted I asked Chris if he wanted me to intervene.

"No, Mom. I can handle it." Chris was emphatic that I didn't rescue him. He was right. He needed to gain respect on his own. And it wasn't long before he did. However, his attendance was so limited he didn't get much of a chance to bond with anyone.

Around that time his old buddy "Tommy" came back into his life. Not long before the fall term started we had run into Tommy and his family at a local pizza parlor. As soon as Chris spotted his old friend he went over and sat down with him. The two of them talked and laughed just like old times. I smiled and waved, but didn't say much. I was still hurt over them never visiting Chris in the hospital.

I found out later that Tommy's parents had never told their son about Chris's leukemia. Finally, after seeing Chris without a hair on his head, they'd had to tell Tommy the truth. I was seething. "What, my kid's diseased, so he's not good enough for your kid any more? What cowards!" I thought. "And how sad that they had denied their Tommy the opportunity to show compassion, the opportunity to witness Chris's bravery."

But I knew I had to put my personal feelings aside for Chris's sake. Tommy was in several of Chris's classes at school, so his reentry into Chris's life was well timed. With the little bit Chris was able to attend school he needed a friend sitting next to him in class. Once the ice was broken Tommy's family made an effort to resume our friendship. So we had to give them credit for learning from their mistakes.

That fall Chris made a new friend at the hospital as well. It was the first time since Jo Jo that he had reached out to someone.

September 8, 2000

... Started chemo about 4:00 PM. Chris had a lot of fun hanging out with Jeremy (a lymphoma patient about the same age as Chris). They are very compatible. We are training Jeremy to pick on Nurse Nancy. We told him how much she enjoys blonde jokes ... Later they moved Jeremy into Chris's room and the two of them had a nice afternoon together. They went to the playroom for a while, and played video games and shot spitballs at the nurses. It was great to hear their laughter ...

By evening Chris was nauseous and the fun was over. I tried to imagine what it must feel like to be sick so much. Like having regularly scheduled bouts with the flu or living with chronic morning sickness. Sometimes even the smell of food made Chris vomit. On many occasions Bob or I had gone out to get Chris fast food and returned only to find him too ill to eat it.

The next day was Jarrod's seventh birthday. And once again, I found myself torn between two worlds.

September 9, 2000

I went for a run, did my RMH chore and got up to Chris's room around 9:45. He was just waking up and feeling OK until about 10:30. The nurse gave him some ativan for his nausea, and I waited for it to kick in before I left for Sarasota to go to Jarrod's party. Just what I felt like doing, spending the afternoon in a crowded arcade with a bunch of six- and seven-year-olds, smiling, taking pictures, pretending everything's normal. Well, at least Jarrod had fun, and I knew I had to be there for him. But all that noise and commotion! I couldn't wait to get back up to the hospital where I didn't have to wear a fake smile.

I brought Chris and Jeremy back some Silly String. Chris's feet and back were hurting from his chemo, so we decided to sic Jeremy on Nurse Nancy. He did an outstanding job dousing her ...

Somewhere over the long months of treatment a strange transformation had taken place in my attitude about the hospital. It now felt more like home than my home. I had become acclimated to the culture there. I knew a large number of the staff by sight if not by name. I knew the access codes to the ambulance entrance (a great short-cut), and the nurses' nutrition room where they kept the snacks and the ice machine. I knew that the snack cart lady would save Chris's favorite snacks for him, and I knew Miss Lucy, the sweet elderly transport tech who was the longest standing employee and had been there since the hospital opened. I knew Barbara in the admissions office liked dirty jokes. I knew Miss Mary the housekeeper would leap back in shock when she spotted Chris's gag rubber dog poop that he would place on the floor, but she'd be laughing hysterically a minute later. I knew I could go hang out in the schoolroom with Gail, the hospital schoolteacher and she'd let me bitch and moan. Most importantly, I knew I didn't have to pretend everything was all right.

That's what it felt like when I was at home nowadays, like a big pretense. I went through the motions of being the good wife, mother, and schoolteacher, but I always felt a sense of responsibility to remain strong and conceal my pain. I know Bob, being the main breadwinner, probably felt it even more so.

12

A SPECIAL FAMILY

In October I became reacquainted with a family I hadn't seen in years. Earlier in my teaching career I had the honor of knowing the Rogers (names changed) family. Back in 1987 this family made national news when it was discovered that three of their four children were HIV positive. At the time there was little public awareness of AIDS and HIV. Fueled by fear and ignorance some of their so-called neighbors had burned down their house and driven them out of their hometown. They came to Sarasota, and eight-year-old Danny was enrolled in my third-grade classroom.

A few days before their arrival a team of doctors and medical experts were sent to our school to answer our questions. The teachers and guidance counselors spoke to all the students ahead of time, assuring them that they weren't going to catch anything and it was perfectly OK to play with the Rogers boys. Despite this thoughtful preparation there were still some parents who objected, and for a while our school parking lot was a media circus of reporters and huge satellite trucks.

I told my class I was proud of them because the eyes of the world were upon them and I knew that they would make Danny feel welcome. Then the guidance counselor brought in a sandy haired, round-faced little boy, and within an hour he was on the floor working a puzzle and chatting with the other students. The media frenzy was temporarily forgotten as the children got down to the more important business of making friends and hoping that Mrs. Ditmars would extend the playtime a little longer that day.

I watched as the Rogers family struggled to remain what they really were—just an ordinary family. An ordinary family under extraordinary circumstances, their three boys dealing with a life-threatening illness, and suddenly being thrust into national attention as the poster children for a new awareness.

Danny took his fame in stride. For show and tell he brought in autographed photos of celebrities and sports figures, but he didn't let it go to his head. Like most children he was open and honest, and he explained to the class that he had hemophilia, a bleeding disorder. He and his brothers had become HIV infected from tainted blood products used to treat the hemophilia. (That was before blood products were tested.) Sometimes he would get nosebleeds and he would calmly excuse himself to the health room.

For the most part, the Sarasota community welcomed the Rogers with open arms, but unpleasant incidents still occurred. When someone started a vicious rumor that Danny was deliberately spitting on other children trying to infect them I saw the tears of anger and frustration in his parents' eyes. His mom, Lynn, held her head up and stayed involved in the classroom, going on field trips with us. Danny followed her example and tried to ignore the taunts and lies, but it hurt, and sometimes he had to stick up for himself. I admired his spunk.

The following year I had the pleasure of teaching Danny's sister, Cindy, who was not HIV infected. She was cheerful and cooperative and wasn't jealous of the attention her brothers received. She was very protective of them.

In a few short years, their oldest brother, Phillip, was dead. Phillip's funeral was the first time I had ever seen a child laid to rest. Once again, I admired the Rogers for their courage.

I thought of that family a lot over the years, especially after Chris was diagnosed and I discovered that the Rogers boys had also been treated by Dr. Barbosa at All Children's Hospital. The Rogers had become a role model for me in my efforts to deal with Chris's illness. Despite the adversities they faced, they never forgot how to laugh and play and just be little boys. I had always encouraged Chris to do the same.

Over the years I had heard that the Rogers had moved out of Florida, and the surviving boys, Danny and Jason were doing OK. I was half right.

October 5, 2000

… I was sitting in Chris's hospital room talking to Bobby on the phone. He was at home leafing through the Sarasota paper. He spotted an article about Jason Rogers, and he read it to me. Apparently Jason wasn't doing well, and the family had returned to Florida to seek medical treatment for him. Then I hung up, went downstairs to stretch my legs, and literally ran into Mr. Rogers in the hallway. He didn't remember me at first, but Lynn recognized me immediately. She said that she had seen Chris's name on the board by the nurses' station and had wondered if it was the same Ditmars that they knew. Wow, it's been years since I've seen them.

She reported that Jason's condition was serious and he was in ICU. Cindy, the youngest, was now nineteen, married, and in school to be a teacher. Both Danny and Jason were engaged. I updated them on Chris …

So now, ironically, our paths crossed once again. This time my role was vastly altered. I was no longer their children's teacher. Now I was a fellow parent also struggling with my child's life in the balance. Never could I have imagined that our reunion would be under such circumstances.

A few days later Jason made it out of ICU, and he was moved to a room just two doors down from Chris. I was able to see the kids, and I was amazed at how wonderful Danny looked. He was tall and muscular, and he reported that he was symptom-free. I wondered what must be going through his mind as he sat next to his sick brother.

In the meantime Chris was having a rough week. He was extremely depressed and didn't want to get out of bed. He was crying for long periods of time and saying how much he hated his life. It was emotionally exhausting trying to come up with things to say to make him feel better.

Dr. Grana sent the pediatric psychiatrist, Dr. Cole, up to see him. During our conversation I asked Dr. Cole to check Chris's medical orders, and we discovered that Chris hadn't been receiving his antidepressant!

Someone in the clinic had failed to list the antidepressant in the orders that were sent over to the hospital. No wonder Chris had crashed emotionally. I was angry, and I marched over to the clinic and gave Dr. Barbosa an earful.

I learned two important things from the experience: First, Chris was definitely benefiting from the antidepressants, and second, always check the orders to make sure the meds are right.

A few days later Chris made it home, and was able to stay home for two weeks before his next scheduled inpatient treatment. Once his counts recovered we had a few good days before we had to head back to the hospital. He and Bobby enjoyed father-son lunches and movies together, and I spent some quality time with Chris also.

"Mom, forget about cleaning up," he'd say after everyone else was in bed. "Why don't you make us some soft pretzels and we'll sit on the sofa and watch a movie." So for a couple of blissful hours the big, bad, disease-ridden world would disappear, and there would just be a mom and her son hanging out together.

During his time at home we still had our weekly outpatient clinic visits. On one of those days I asked Chris if he wanted to go over to the hospital afterward and visit Jason Rogers. After running into them again I couldn't stop thinking about them. Jason's out-of-state doctors had given up on him. Dr. Barbosa was their last shot. At home I had gone through my old school yearbooks and found several pictures of the Rogers children. I had made copies and wanted to give them to Lynn.

It was the time of year that all of the Halloween items were in the stores. Chris had purchased a sheet of rather ghoulish and gruesome temporary tattoos. The day of our visit Chris had pasted a tattoo of a blood-spattered bullet hole right smack in the middle of his bald head. "Gee, that's really attractive, honey," I commented, "that'll cheer him right up."

In the clinic, Chris lay down on the examining table and waited for the nurse to enter. When she did he moaned loudly, "I've been shot, Ahhhhhhh."

"He seems to have quite a headache," I deadpanned. "We're not sure why."

"Well, I guess we'll have to admit you, then," the nurse laughed.

"Wait, it's a miracle! I'm all better." Chris grinned and sat up.

Chris enjoyed parading around with his "injury" on our way up to Jason's room. Of course, everyone knew Chris so well that no one seemed particularly alarmed that he appeared to have a dripping hole in his head. "We could stagger around in the ER for a while," I offered.

When we got up to Jason's room he was surrounded by family, and at first I hesitated, thinking that it wasn't a good time. But Lynn waved for us to come in. The room was dark and Jason looked exhausted, but he was alert. Lynn spoke softly and told me that Jason was looking forward to being in Heaven with Phillip.

I handed her the pictures, and she smiled with delight at one photo of all four of the children sitting on Santa's lap. "I think I'm going to use that one for my Christmas cards this year," she said.

Then Jason spotted Chris's bullet hole and laughed so hard that his oxygen mask almost fell off. It was the last time we saw Jason alive.

I like to think that we had given them the best gift possible—some cherished memories and a good laugh. But what really happened was that they had actually given us a great gift. They had allowed us a glimpse of their incredible faith in God and their wonderful love for each other.

13

LAUGHTER AND TEARS

We began the month of November with a fever admit. Chris was put on IV antibiotics and morphine. For several days his temperature fluctuated between 100 and 104 degrees. He suffered from frequent diarrhea and he tested positive for bacteria in his stool. On top of that his back was hurting again. These were all side effects of the chemo and the low counts.

When he wasn't in the bathroom Chris slept as much as possible. When he slept I caught up on my sleep, and I e-mailed Barb who sent me a folder full of blonde jokes. When I couldn't bear to sit around any longer watching Chris attempt to snooze away his misery, I'd prowl the halls armed with my very bad jokes.

Usually I'd approach the nurses' station with the intent of annoying Nurse Nancy. She would pretend to ignore me as I said something like, "Nancy, did you hear about the blonde who stared at the carton of orange juice for thirty minutes because it said 'concentrate'?" Nancy would then make a face while everyone else would laugh. It wasn't as much fun as hearing Chris fling jokes at her, but it was a good way for me to dispel some nervous energy.

Some days I was like a fire hydrant full of emotion that had to be let out. It didn't always matter what the emotion was. Laughter was often a good substitute for tears. It was my antidote for living in a community of death.

November 5, 2000

A family staying at RMH lost their son today. The house is quiet and grief hangs in the air thick like the Florida humidity. There is so much death here. I have to try to think of this place as an angel factory, and I hope Chris isn't ready for processing any time soon ... In the hall I saw Wesley's dad today. (He's the bone marrow transplant patient whose mom I helped with her insurance paperwork.) Wesley is in ICU, in a coma. He's bleeding in his lungs and kidneys ...

A few days later Wesley died. It was his ninth birthday.

Chris was able to come home for only six days before his next chemo admit. He was now in the second part of cycle six in his eight-cycle protocol. Each cycle consisted of two chemotherapy hospitalizations. Of course, that didn't include the unscheduled treatments for fevers and side effects. For the best treatment results it was important that we adhere to the schedule as closely as possible. If Chris had to spend some of his recovery time in the hospital instead of at home he wasn't allowed to make up the lost days at home.

But with only two cycles left we could see the light at the end of the tunnel. We would be done with the inpatient portion of his treatments by the end of February. Chris could finally start thinking about the future again. Nonetheless, we couldn't forget that Chris's relapse had greatly reduced his odds for survival.

November 16, 2000

They hung Chris's second bag of MTX at 3:45 PM. Chris slept a lot then perked up around dinnertime. We went down to the cafeteria and split a chicken Parmesan dinner. On the way out Chris, as usual, paused to place a lemon slice on the toaster rack so it would sizzle. And of course, I pretended I didn't see him.

Later, back in the room Chris said, "I love you, Mom. I'll always love you no matter what. If anything happens I'll be your guardian angel. I'll be the guardian angel for the whole family and I'll be looking down on you."

Chris didn't hide from his mortality. He confronted it head-on. He had already seen so much death in his young life that he had wisely begun to assimilate his own vision of Heaven and angels. He had decided that if he did die he might as well choose his own angelic career—watching over us.

While such discussions were frightening, they were also uplifting and spiritual. Chris didn't just wish for a better place, he *knew* there was a better place, and he wasn't afraid to talk about it. I was enormously grateful for his faith and openness. I knew that it was vitally important to have these conversations no matter what happened. If he lived he would feel loved and protected, and if he didn't he could look forward to going to a place where his spirit would be loved and protected. I felt as if he had a special connection to a divine wisdom.

Sometimes I talked with the other moms about such matters. Some of the other children had special angels that they spoke about, and like Chris, they dealt openly with their mortality. Other parents told me that they never discussed death with their children. I had known children who passed and never had the opportunity to talk about an afterlife. After being around children for so many years as both a teacher and a mom, I knew that just about all children, healthy or otherwise, thought about it. I felt that the ones who were encouraged to speak openly with their families were far richer for the experience. I couldn't imagine not having those conversations.

Drugs and pain management and medications continued to be an issue. During this admit both Dr. Rossbach and Nurse Nancy expressed concern over Chris's frequent requests for pain meds.

November 17, 2000

*... Dr. Rossbach came in and spoke to Chris for quite a while. He was concerned about Chris not getting out of bed enough, and always asking for ativan. Chris was also frequently asking the nurses to push it (push the stopper on the syringe to quickly administer the drug rather than allowing it to finish on the pump). Dr. Rossbach told Chris about kids he knew who went through treatment and ended up drug dependent. He's taking Chris off the IV ativan and putting him on PO (by mouth) benadryl. I told Chris that the doctors would be more inclined to give him pain drugs if they saw him up and about and not just waiting for his next dose. *Sigh* So much to deal with!*

After Dr. Rossbach's talk I got Chris to go to the playroom for a while. We played bumper pool for a while and he called me "Mrs. Bumperdoodles." Then Chris went out on the rooftop playground with Ethan from child-life and did some pottery ...

While Chris was gone I thoroughly enjoyed bombarding Nancy with blonde jokes. She said that after a day with the Ditmars she has to go out drinking, then take four days off to recover.

With Chris in the hospital so much we tried to bring up Erin and Jarrod to see him whenever possible, but it wasn't always a pleasant experience. Erin was now eighteen and a senior. She had a busy class schedule, was working, and had a boyfriend. She was always in a hurry to get to work or some all-important social engagement. It hurt me that she wasn't more attentive to Chris, and we had more than one argument about it, but we reached a compromise. Chris and Erin's boyfriend, Jose, got along well, and they both shared a common interest in video games. He was like a big brother to Chris. So most of the time Jose and Erin came to visit Chris together. They were free to leave on their own, and Chris was usually tired by the time they left. Erin liked the freedom and the fact that we treated her and Jose as a couple.

Jarrod presented a different type of challenge when we brought him. He had always been hyperactive and full of energy. This was difficult to manage in the confines of a hospital room, and after a while Jarrod would end up annoying Chris.

November 18, 2000

... Bobby and Jarrod came up around noon. Jarrod was his usual nonstop self. I took Jarrod to the arts and crafts program at RMH so Bobby could have some quiet time with Chris ... When we came back into the room later Jarrod was turning up the TV loud and pestering Chris, so I took Jarrod back to RMH again ...

That's how it usually went when Jarrod was around. One of us would stay with Chris while the other one entertained Jarrod. We would bring him into Chris's room for a short visit then trot off somewhere else so Jarrod could blow off some of his energy.

One of Jarrod's favorite activities was riding a wagon or a wheelchair across the pedestrian bridge that separated the hospital from the medical office building. The bridge was angled slightly, which made it even more fun. Someone in his or her infinite institutional and architectural wisdom had decided to connect the second floor of the hospital to the third floor of the office building. This meant that, with a good push, one could enjoy a high-speed coast from the higher end.

We would wait until no one was around and I'd push him off. He would sail toward the door at the lower end and just before crashing into the doors he'd reach out and punch the metal button on the wall. The doors would open just in time for Jarrod to zip through. If anyone saw him I'd act surprised and say, "Young man, do your parents know that you're doing that?"

More often than not, one of us would just stay home with Jarrod.

Chris was able to remain at home until his next scheduled admission in early December. There were no major problems, and Chris felt well enough to entertain us all with some of his pranks.

December 7, 2000

... During the video bingo game Chris kept calling the extension, and instead of reporting a winning bingo card like the other callers he kept hitting on the female child-life counselors. He disguised his voice and asked them out on dates, promising them the time of their lives. They just laughed and said, "We know it's you, Chris!"

Later, when the nurse came in to give Chris his leg shot she asked him which leg she should inject. Chris quickly pointed to her leg and said, "That one!" ...

Unfortunately, the rest of December was miserable. Five days after going home Chris was back in the hospital with severe mucositis.

December 13, 2000

Chris has been feeling awful the last couple of days—mucositis sores everywhere. He's having difficulty swallowing and eating. Bobby took Chris up to the clinic this morning, and by the time they got there Chris had a fever of 102.5. He couldn't even walk from the car to the clinic, and he was throwing up phlegm.

I arrived around 7:30 PM, and Bobby reported that there was some concern about Chris getting pneumonia or becoming septic. His ANC is zero, and he looks awful. He's pale, sweating profusely, and coughing.

Nurse Brenda said that the coughing was actually good. It gets the infection out. They will get Chris up every few hours during the night to make sure he keeps coughing it up.

… When Bobby said the word "septic" I immediately thought of Michael Olson. Funny, I just got a Christmas card from his mom … Well, Angel Michael; we have some work for you.

For the next week Chris was extremely ill. After running tests they determined that he had an infection in his port. This was not uncommon with cancer patients, but nonetheless it had to be treated aggressively with antibiotics. Since his counts were zero he had no ability to fight the infection on his own. That combined with his coughing and mucositis was very worrisome.

As is often the case with low counts, transfusions of blood products were required. Chris received both platelets and packed red cells. Without the platelets he would have been in danger of serious bleeding, and the red cells would boost his hemoglobin.

Chris also had other abnormal blood tests. They indicated that he was in need of IV nutrition. In addition to that Dr. Grana reported that Chris had the worst mucositis she'd seen in him. I thanked God for his morphine pump.

Early in the morning on the seventeenth the nurses called us over at RMH while we were sleeping.

December 17, 2000

About 4:30 AM Sharon called to tell us that Chris's O2 sats (short for oxygen saturation level—the measure of how much oxygen he was absorbing into his lungs) were very low. She thought that one of us should come over. They were running tests to see if Chris had pneumonia …

... Later: Sats keep going down! They have to keep turning up his oxygen. The respiratory doctor examined Chris and ordered more tests ...

Later, they did confirm pneumonia, and Chris had to endure back-pounding therapy, which was very painful for him. Afterward he would cough and throw up, but he never complained.

And just when I'd swear that I was absolutely at my wit's end I'd get a small gift that would keep me going. My boss, Marilyn, and my fellow fourth-grade teachers called and sang their very own rendition of "Jingle Bells." It went like this: "Christmas sucks, Christmas sucks, It sucks all the way ..." It was the best music I'd heard in ages!

They weren't the only ones thinking of us.

December 18, 2000

... Making it home for Christmas is looking iffy, so I asked Judy at RMH where to go in town to get some Christmas decorations for Chris's room. "Don't you dare buy a thing!" she proclaimed, "Wait right here." Then she disappeared downstairs in the storeroom, and emerged five minutes later with armloads of Christmas decorations. There was a small tree with battery-powered lights, garland, ornaments, stuffed animals, and three stockings fully stuffed—one for each of our kids ... Some of the small ornaments doubled nicely for earrings!

After that Chris started to improve. He was being successful in coughing up his infection, and his mucositis had subsided. His old buddy "Tommy" and his dad came to visit, and Chris really enjoyed seeing him. Chris was now able to sit up and talk for a while, but he still tired very easily. He wasn't able to converse much, and I hoped that they understood.

By the twentieth Chris was showing very rapid improvement, and we now had a reasonable expectation of being home for Christmas. But the challenges just continued to follow us. The day before Chris was scheduled to be released I was in Sarasota with Jarrod Christmas shopping. We had been up at the hospital with Chris that morning, then gone to the mall. I was exhausted. As I was putting the packages down on the kitchen counter, Jarrod suddenly screamed. He had managed to slice his finger open with a butcher knife, and there was blood everywhere!

I hate to admit it, but as I applied pressure to his finger I wasn't thinking, "You poor thing," I was thinking, "No, no more trips to the hospital today!" So I sent Erin to the drug store for butterfly bandages and patched it up myself.

My trip home with Chris proved even more eventful. He did indeed get discharged before Christmas, but we were required to finish his IV antibiotics at home. They left his port accessed with tubing extending out. We were instructed how to do the infusions which actually wasn't a difficult process and definitely worth doing in order to get home for Christmas. A home health nurse would meet us at home to walk us through the first procedure. So we headed out for what we thought would be a peaceful ride home.

December 21, 2000

... Right after Chris was discharged we were on Fourth Street waiting to turn left and a man ran a red light, t-boned a car in the intersection, and that car spun into me, smashing the left front of my van. It happened in an instant. We were shaken, but not hurt. This getting home for Christmas business is getting quite complicated ... So it was another very long day. My wheel axle was broken so we had to be towed all the way back to Sarasota, then I had to deal with juggling getting a rental and scheduling the home health nurse. I became quite assertive with the rental company and insisted that they drop off the vehicle at our house. It's a lot easier to be bitchy these days ...

We had done it—made it home for Christmas, and we were all together. Our tree was in the living room by the sliders that led out to our pool area, and underneath was a colorful pile of gifts, just like in so many other households. Chris felt well, and we could all sit around the tree and open our presents. But being together was the greatest gift of all, for this would be our last Christmas all together.

14

ARE WE REALLY DONE?

January 1, 2001

Happy New Year. We brought Chris in to start his chemo today so we could get him out in time to watch me run the Disney Half Marathon. We had a good Christmas week. Chris had fun playing with his cousins and zipping around the neighborhood on his motorized scooter ...

... It's a lot more fun being in the hospital when Chris feels well. He was in rare form entertaining the nurses with his silly voices, noises, and faces. Chris also amused everyone by saving files on the laptop and having it say them out loud. So when someone walked into his room they heard the computer say, "Saving: I just farted, and it smells."

There was a new nurse on the floor today so we initiated her with our rubber vomit. It was great fun watching her surprised reaction when she tried to wipe it up ...

Other than high blood pressure, which was a common side effect for Chris, he had no ill effects. The blood pressure was brought down by medication, and Chris was able to eat and remain active for the remainder of his stay. It was quite a contrast from the last time when he had pneumonia and didn't eat for seven days.

Chris didn't ask for a lot of pain meds this time, either. Bobby and I discussed this and the doctor's previous concerns about Chris being addicted. We were delighted that Chris was comfortable without them, but we felt that his behavior during this admission was an indicator that he really wasn't addicted. After all, if he really were addicted he would continue to ask for the painkillers. This made us wonder if they would take care of him properly when he really was in pain. Bobby and I both agreed that we were more concerned with Chris's pain being managed properly than whether or not he was addicted. As Bobby said, "So what if he's hooked? He has cancer. We can worry about getting him off of that stuff later. Right now we're just trying to keep him alive and comfortable."

Fortunately we didn't have to face that issue this time. Chris was released on Thursday the fourth, and we went to Orlando for the weekend. I had signed up for the Disney Half Marathon as another Team in Training event. Once again Bob and I had fund-raised for cancer research in Chris's honor. This time we had raised over $3,000.00.

Chris felt well that weekend, and we were able to enjoy the hotel and the theme parks, but the main attraction was definitely the marathon. Chris hadn't been with us when we ran The Dublin Marathon, so this was an opportunity to see his mom in action. He was also present at the banquet the night before, and was able to meet many of the runners who were participating in his honor. They wore hospital bracelets with Chris's name on them.

Standing at the finish line waiting for me to finish, he could see firsthand, the tears and the sweat. And just as we had witnessed as spectators the year before, Chris saw hundreds of runners wearing the distinctive purple TNT singlets, and he knew that they were running to help save the lives of cancer patients like him. Out of the 18,000 runners participating, 3,300 were Team in Training runners, and the event raised over $7,000, 000 for cancer research.

We were proud and grateful to be a part of all of that. I think meeting the runners made Chris feel like the hero that he was, and seeing a banquet hall filled with thousands of TNT runners reminded him how many people cared. The experience made me feel like a hero as well.

I remembered running through EPCOT just before sunrise, with the sky just beginning to brighten, and the buildings around a huge lake were lit up like Christmas. All of the restaurants in the park had their various countries' ethnic music playing on loudspeakers, and costumed employees smiled and waved as we trotted by. It felt as if the whole entire world was cheering for us.

Near the finish we ran into the Magic Kingdom, right through Cinderella's Castle and down Main Street, USA. I had scanned a picture of Chris and made a sign that read: "Hi, I'm Maribeth from Sarasota. I'm running for my son, Chris, who has been winning the fight against leukemia since '97." I wore the sign on my race singlet and the crowd along Main Street called out my name and words of encouragement about Chris. The Disney Characters were there, too, and I imagined all of their Disney magic being part of our prayers for Chris's cure.

By February Chris had only one more scheduled chemotherapy hospitalization remaining. There were no major problems, but near the end of his stay he started developing mucositis again, so we decided not to celebrate prematurely. We knew from experience that there was a good chance he'd have to come back one more time for pain and fever management.

At the end of the last few admits we sometimes had to assert ourselves a bit regarding Chris's pain medication. We would have to argue to get an adequate prescription for pain medication at home. I supposed that doctors were probably under a lot of pressure not to overmedicate their patients and have them end up addicted, but Chris had gained weight from the steroids he was on, and he had become very narcotic tolerant. In our opinion, one or two of the doctors didn't comprehend Chris's needs. Some of them were prescribing him the same dose he'd had back in 1998 when he was thirty pounds lighter. We were the ones who lived with Chris, and saw how a couple of Tylenol 3s would enable him to get out of bed and sit at the dinner able with his family. They saw a teenager who wanted pills.

Fortunately, not all of the doctors were deaf to our concerns, and if one doctor refused we approached another one who tended to be more sympathetic. On the release days Chris would look on the board by the nurses' station to see who the on-call doctor was. If it was one of the stingy ones we'd know we were in for a battle. Sometimes we went home with a prescription that we knew was inadequate, and we'd call the clinic a few days later, hoping to get a different doctor. A few times we bypassed the on-call doctor and went directly to the head oncologist, Dr. Barbosa, who was reasonable and compassionate.

Another incident that month reinforced our position that Chris wasn't requesting unnecessary pain medication. During one of his good days he was out on his scooter and he fell on his arm. He came into the house saying it hurt, but he didn't seem to be in great distress. There was no apparent cut or swelling. But a day and a half later he was still complaining and saying that it was keeping him up at night. So we took him up to the hospital to have it x-rayed, and we discovered that it was broken in two places!

The poor kid had slept two nights on an untreated broken arm because he'd grown so accustomed to pain. We felt terrible that we hadn't had it x-rayed immediately, but we also realized that Chris had developed a high pain tolerance. In my opinion it was a clear indicator that when Chris did claim to be hurting he deserved to be taken quite seriously. The doctors didn't question Chris's need for pain meds for his broken arm, so why did they question him when he was having bone pain from chemotherapy?

Overall, Chris received outstanding care at All Children's, but I still harbor some resentment regarding this issue. We shouldn't have had to beg for adequate meds; after almost four years of treatment we felt that we deserved more trust than that. When dealing with a patient with a deadly disease, health care professionals need to look at the big picture. They need to consider the patient's quality of life outside the hospital setting. In such extreme cases as Chris's, addiction issues should be bumped further down the list of concerns.

But hopefully, that would all be behind us soon. Having reached the end of the high dose portion of Chris's second protocol I once again had those strange mixed feelings: a combination of joy, fear, and separation anxiety. We were very excited to be done with twelve months of intense chemotherapy, but it was that same chemotherapy that had knocked Chris back in remission for the second time. Would he be OK on the lower doses?

On the other hand, life wouldn't be worth living if he had to continue forever on his current protocol. So we had to forge ahead, and pray and hope for the best. We were encouraged by what the doctors said: Chris was still in remission, and his brain scans showed no further damage from the MTX. We also continued to draw courage from all of the kind people around us.

In early February I was given the opportunity to say thank you to some of those kind people: all of the staff and volunteers at the three Tampa Bay area Ronald McDonald Houses. They invited me to bring the family and be the keynote speaker at their annual luncheon. They wanted me to tell Chris's story, and speak about the positive impact that the RMH had had on our lives. I was honored to have such an opportunity.

Judy and Sally Jo from RMH told me that the luncheon had a tacky tourist, Key West theme. They were enjoying hunting up Hawaiian shirts, flowery hats, and all sorts of tropical knickknacks. I asked them how they were set for earrings. "You know I have a collection of about four hundred. If you like, I could be your earring consultant and loan you some."

They loved the idea, so I brought in a Ziploc bag filled with dozens of my tackiest baubles. I had earrings that resembled hula girls, tropical birds, palm trees, flip-flops, sunglasses, margarita glasses, and more. When the time came to stand at the podium and speak to a room filled with RMH staff and volunteers, I felt at ease because everywhere I looked I saw my earrings!

In addition to telling Chris's story and expressing our appreciation for all that they had done, I decided to tell them the tale of Ollie Klump. Ollie was a bit of a secret, and even Chris hadn't heard of him.

Each family that stays at RMH is required to do a daily chore, as well as clean their own rooms, as there is no maid service. The chores were assigned by room number, and there was a chart on the refrigerator where you marked your initials when you were finished the chore. Our favorite room, 35, had a vacuuming chore.

When I was staying there I was a good girl and always did my chore, I told them, but Bob, well, he was a bit of a chore slacker. He'd gaze at the hallway that had just been vacuumed the day before, and quite often he'd come to the conclusion that it really didn't need to be vacuumed again so soon. So rather than be dishonest by placing his initials on the chart, Bob would write "O.K." As he put it, "I was acknowledging the fact that the chore existed, but I decided it looked O.K." This was where Ollie Klump came in. You see, that was the name we had given our fictitious benefactor, Ollie Klump, whose initials were "O.K."!

Now that we weren't going to be staying at the house any more, we felt that it was only fair to leave Ollie behind so that he could help other families.

We were right not to celebrate too soon. Four days after Chris came home he was back in the hospital with a fever. As was customary with fevers, Chris was put on IV antibiotics and they ran blood cultures to check for bacterial infections. Chris slept a lot for two days, then on the third day he perked up.

Chris challenged me to a championship match of bumper-pool, and he also amused himself by running his remote control truck up and down the halls. I'm sure that the kitchen workers pushing the huge carts full of food trays thoroughly enjoyed having a small jeep run over their toes.

As I wrote in my journal I wondered if it would really be my last hospital entry.

February 22, 2001

... *Are we really done? Back and forth to the hospital has become our life. It's a strange feeling to want so badly to be done, but to also be afraid of the future.*

Here's a list of things I'll miss the most: Pestering Nurse Nancy with dumb blonde jokes, and referring to her as "Smelly Melly," playing bumper pool with Chris on his good days and hearing him call me "Mrs. Bumperdoodles," the many pranks Chris played on the staff especially goofing on the child-life staff at video bingo, all of the wonderful staff and volunteers at both the hospital and the RMH ... Things I won't miss: Chris's pain, diarrhea, vomit, Chris's tears of longing for a normal life, seeing children die—watching that downcast look when nurses aren't allowed to tell you that someone a few doors away has passed, hearing Chris ask, "Am I going to die too?"

I also made a list of all the children I knew who had passed, and all of those who had survived and done well. The first list was longer.

15

SHORT-LIVED REMISSION

Ever so gingerly we opened the door that led to the rest of our lives. Once again we allowed ourselves to hope and plan for the future. Chris was now back on his once-a-week clinic schedule. He would go in, get a leg shot of methotrexate, have his counts checked, and we were usually out of there in less than forty-five minutes.

It didn't take long for him to start feeling better, and he started back at school. He still took oral chemotherapy medicine at night that compromised his energy level somewhat, but he was back in the mainstream of life again.

All of us were back in the mainstream again, but we were changed forever. Maybe it's the same renewed sense of appreciation felt by a released hostage, or someone who's had a near-death experience. Nothing would ever feel, smell, or taste exactly the same again. It was an amazing opportunity to start a new segment of life that had a richer, sweeter flavor.

Chris's comments reflected this appreciation. "Mom, stop cleaning the kitchen, it looks fine. Let's make popcorn and watch a movie." Or, referring to the students at his middle school, "Those kids just don't know how lucky they are, do they, Mom?" Probably the comment that touched me the most was, "I love my house and my room."

With the doctors' approval we decided to take a trip out west with Grandmommy and Granddaddy. We chose the Las Vegas area because of its close proximity to many beautiful landforms and parks. Also, my parents had never been to that part of the country. It would be a seven-day ramble between Nevada and Arizona.

We opted to go during spring break when school was out, but Erin begged to stay home. She was now eighteen and a senior. Since we live in a beach resort area, spring break was a big deal for seniors. It had been more than a year since her infamous party, so we decided to give her another chance. Also, we realized that she had missed out on a lot due to Chris's long treatment schedule.

It would become a special bonding time for Chris and his grandparents. The first two days were spent on beautiful Lake Mead. We rented a room in a lakefront motel on the Arizona side. We explored the impressive canyons and waterways by boat, and Chris even had the energy to climb atop a giant sand dune. In the evening we sat out on the front patio and watched as the spectacular sunsets painted pastel hues on the canyon walls.

We also toured the Hoover Dam, and were awestruck by power of the giant water driven generators, and the steep angles of the cable towers. Chris and Jarrod enjoyed setting and resetting their watches as we drove back and forth across the Nevada and Arizona state line, which also separated the Mountain and Pacific Time zones.

The following day we drove through the desert dotted with beautiful yellow and purple wildflowers. We took a raft trip through the Black Canyon and gazed at tiny, steaming waterfalls created by subterranean hot springs. Jarrod pointed with delight when we spotted a herd of wild rams scampering over the rocks. The two largest males battled for leadership. You could hear the clack of their horns echo off the canyon walls.

Another day we drove into the mountains, exchanging the heat of the desert for snowy roads winding through a pine forest. It was amazing to watch the land transform itself from barren desert to snowy mountains.

When we went into Las Vegas we decided to break a few rules. Amid the glitz and bell-ringing we snuck Chris and Jarrod into a casino. Jarrod was small enough to hide behind us, and we formed a protective circle around Chris, hoping no one would notice. If anyone glanced our way Grandmommy quickly scooted in front of Chris, obscuring him from prying eyes. We laughed like naughty school children as Chris yanked the one-armed bandit, watching the cherries and apples zoom past. A giggling Jarrod reached his little arm up from underneath scooping up quarters. We grew bold and careless, telling Chris that if he won a car we'd get him a fake ID and let him drive it down the strip.

Then the quarters were gone, and we were surrounded by security guards. Our three generations of conspirators were escorted out of the casino. "Well, I never!" clucked an indignant female security guard.

We just grinned and said, "Well, we did!"

In the meantime Chris had started complaining about his left arm and shoulder aching. He had just had his arm cast taken off, and we wondered if he had refractured it. (The large doses of steroids given to cancer patients can weaken bones.) Just to be sure we took him to him to the local hospital for an x-ray.

There was no break. They gave Chris some painkillers and told us to have him checked when we got home.

The pain pills did the trick, and we knew we'd be home in a couple of days. Surely everything would be OK. Our last night we took the boys to see Siegfried and Roy, and Chris was captivated. It was an evening of smoky magic and disappearing tigers. I remember thinking that maybe Chris would get to do a magic show for Jarrod's class this year.

After the show Chris asked to speak to me in private. "Mom, I think it's cancer. I think my leukemia is back."

"Oh, Chris," I said, "I've never heard of anyone relapsing in their arm or shoulder." In truth, relapse can cause bone pain almost anywhere. The shadow of fear crept over me, but I didn't let on to Chris. I thought of how we were on vacation in the Keys when Chris's first symptoms appeared. Now, here we were on vacation again, another delay in getting him to the doctor. The fear mingled with guilt.

God, please don't let it be cancer.

PART IV

THE END OF THE JOURNEY: MARCH 2001–JULY 2001

16

THE MONSTER RETURNS

March 28, 2001

... It was horrible. It took several tries for Dr. Grana and Dr. Kerr to get a successful bone marrow aspiration out of Chris's back. Even with the drugs, fentinol and verset, Chris was groaning while they pushed and twisted the long needle into his bone.

Pacing, pacing, crying, waiting—for what Chris had already known—relapse. Dr. Grana reported 40 percent blasts in his marrow. (That meant 40 percent of the blood in Chris's bone marrow was cancerous.) His only hope for survival is a bone marrow transplant.

Tearfully we discussed transplant options with the doctors. These included stem cell, cord blood, and adult donors ...

It was surreal. Chris wasn't free after all; quite the contrary. Our journey of hope and healing had now twisted treacherously off the planned course. What lay ahead on that dangerous road?

Like last time, notebook in hand, I scrambled for information. Now I had to become knowledgeable about bone marrow transplants. School was back in session; the stakes were higher, and the odds of survival were much lower.

We were given printed materials, and we also had several opportunities to meet with the doctors and the bone marrow nurse. Out of the three possible transplantation methods, the doctors immediately ruled out peripheral (taken from one of your own veins) stem cell transplantation. All blood cells (which are produced in the bone marrow) develop from very immature cells called "stem cells." Most of these cells are contained in the bone marrow, but some circulate in the blood vessels throughout the body. Because these stem cells are so young and undifferentiated, they have the potential to be harvested to form many different types of mature cells. However, since Chris's cancer had significant bone marrow involvement, his stem cells would be much more likely to form new leukemia cells. His new bone marrow would have to come from somewhere else.

The remaining two options were an adult donor, or cord blood. Cord blood is taken from the umbilical cord of a placenta. (The procedure does not harm the newborn in any way.) Since cord blood is rich in stem cells, a high percentage of life-saving stem cells can be harvested from a rather small volume of blood. The disadvantage of cord blood is that it is a one shot deal. If Chris ever needed more, there wouldn't be any. The big advantage with cord blood is that it is so new and pure that there is less chance of rejection than with adult blood cells. Also, with cord blood, the match doesn't have to be as close as it does for adult blood in order for it to work.

The advantage of using adult bone marrow is that a greater volume can be harvested. Also, if Chris needed more cells he could get them. The disadvantage of using an adult donor is that there is a greater chance of rejection (Graft-versus-host disease).

Once again, we had to digest dizzying amounts of information, and once again Chris asked, "Am I going to die?"

"No," I'd responded, "They're just going to give you new bone marrow. Remember Bryce? He had a bone marrow transplant and he's doing fine now."

And like before, I said those things to soothe myself as well as Chris.

March 28, 2001 cont'd

... We had arrived none-too-soon. In the evening Chris became feverish, and was experiencing bone pain. He spiked fevers all night, and was put on morphine ... I just can't believe we are back. What a nightmare ... It was a tearful reunion when we walked back into The Ronald McDonald House. I said, "I thought we were done with this place." The girls all hugged us, and they laughed through their tears when I added, "Well, at least we have Ollie Klump to help out...."

March 29, 2001

I slept poorly last night, went over to RMH to catch a few hours of sleep then stumbled back to Chris's room at 8:00 AM. They had to switch Chris's fluids to bicarb and he was given a drug to keep his potassium from building up. These measures were necessary due to the break down of the leukemic cells ... Poor Chris threw up right when the IV nurse and a student nurse arrived ...

Nurse Ellen brought in a new road map (drug protocol). I can't believe this is his third induction. It's called CCG 1951, and it looks similar to his last one, Cogum. It has a lot of the same drugs. We spoke with Dr. Rossbach for a while:

1. What are your plans for Chris? Ans: Achieve remission, do one month of consolidation, then do a bone marrow transplant. That would be in about six to eight weeks.

2. What do you think are Chris's chances for survival? Ans: About 25 percent.

3. How long do you think he'd live without a transplant? Ans: No more than six months.

4. Are you favoring an adult or cord donor? Ans: We'll have to see what kind of matches we find, then go for the best one. A perfect match isn't necessary.

5. What are the chances of finding a decent match? Ans: Good, about 70 percent.

It was that last piece of information that we focused on when speaking with Chris. He didn't need to hear about his dismal odds for survival. Instinctively, he already knew. After all, he was the one who told us he'd relapsed. The doctors readily admitted that survival odds are just numbers, just educated guesses. So like good salespeople, we quoted the positive statistics like the 70 percent chance of finding a match.

Chris had always had a lot of positive energy, and we intended to help him preserve it. We felt that his upbeat thoughts would have a positive impact on his chances for survival. He never disappointed us when it came to inserting levity into his grim surroundings.

March 29, 2001 cont'd

… Chris reported some blood when wiping himself. It was most likely just a sore from the chemo, but they decided to do a rectal exam to rule out an abscess or an infection. After the doctor left I went back into his room and asked Chris if he was OK. He immediately did a limp-wristed impersonation with a falsetto voice and said (referring to the resident who did the exam) "I think he liked it!"

I laughed for ten minutes … His tests came back normal.

You just never knew what was going to come out of Chris's mouth. Some of the things he said weren't just funny; they were ironic. The day before, when he found out he'd relapsed again, Chris asked us if we thought he'd get another wish (the first had been the Disney Cruise back in 1998).

"Mom, do you think they'll give me another wish?"

"Oh, I don't think so," I had responded, "but it wouldn't hurt to ask."

"Yeah, I'm going to ask them."

"What would you wish for?"

"Well, I can't travel, so I'd want to meet someone famous."

"Who would you pick?"

"Someone really, really big—like God!"

I felt like laughing and crying at the same time, "Oh no, not yet, Chris!"

Afterward, I thought about what Chris had said. Was he just trying to be funny, or was he preparing himself to meet his maker? Perhaps it was a little of both.

The following day Bob and I had a long meeting with Paula, the bone marrow nurse. She explained more about the transplant process and the side effects. After our conversation I had a better understanding of why they had saved bone marrow transplantation as a last resort. It had to be one of the most invasive and hideous things a body could endure.

March 30, 2001

What a sobering meeting we had today with Paula. We learned a lot about the transplant process—mostly how awful it will be. Chris will have to have massive doses of chemotherapy and radiation. He must have his immune system completely destroyed. The radiation is full body including the head. His hospital stay will be about six weeks, and he'll have to remain isolated in a special air-filtered room. There will be numerous precautions that will have to be taken when we are with Chris. She told us to expect significant mucositis as well as some degree of Graft-versus Host Disease.

Before he goes home the house will have to be cleaned throughly from top to bottom. Once he makes it home Chris will need to remain isolated for three or four months. He won't be allowed to attend school for at least eight months ...

After our meeting I couldn't help but wonder if there are some things worse than death. However, we had little time to dwell on those thoughts because when we returned to Chris's room he had a medical emergency.

March 30, 2001 cont'd

... Without warning Chris's temperature and blood pressure suddenly dropped! His BP was only 86/47. Within moments the room was filled with nurses, and they called in Dr. Rossbach. He ordered a bolis (a relatively rapid infusion) of saline, and that brought him back to normal. They had no explanation for the drop, but since his vitals came back up so quickly they weren't too concerned. Well, I was. It scared the heck out of me ... But he was fine after that, and it didn't happen again ...

I wondered if that's what it would be like during the transplant process and the long recovery—sudden, dramatic changes and life-threatening emergencies. I had heard frightening accounts from other families, trips to the ICU and unexpected complications.

After Chris was stabilized he asked me some questions about the transplant. I was honest about the battle before us. "It's going to be tough, buddy, but we know you can do it. We'll be here right beside you every single day. Are you ready to fight?"

Chris had been lying quietly in his bed, tired after his ordeal. He lifted his head slightly off the pillow and said (as if signaling the beginning of a boxing match) "Ding ding."

As the chemo broke down the leukemic cells Chris became more comfortable, but he was tired and not eating much. Despite that, his spirits were good. If he was free from pain, Chris's mood was almost always positive. My parents and my older brother who was visiting from Pennsylvania came to visit, and Chris felt well enough to chat with them. The next day he also felt well enough to play an April fool's joke on the nurses.

April 1, 2001

… We've had quite the April Fool's Day around here. First, Bobby called me and said that our tax return was $15,000.000. As usual, he exaggerated too much and I didn't believe him. I might have bought his story for five grand. His call got Chris and me into an April Foolish spirit so we started scheming.

"Let's freak out the nurses by putting food coloring in your urine! Whaddya think?" I asked.

"Green!" Chris responded.

We were particularly excited because Chris's nurse, Dana, was training a brand-new nurse, Maria, today. There's nothing nicer than fresh bait.

I went over to RMH and raided their cabinets. I confided in Judy and Carla who enthusiastically rummaged alongside me. The best that we could find was pink Jello powder. It would have to do.

As it turned out, it worked quite well. The urine had a lovely hot pink glow. (The urine buckets have little handles on them, and when the patients are done they usually hang them on the board at the foot of the bed so the nurses, who have to record the output, see them.)

In came Dana followed closely by Maria. Chris moaned and pointed to his urinal. We watched as Maria's eyes grew large. But, before she could react, Dana interrupted her. "Let me explain something," she said. "Today is April Fool's Day, and these are the Ditmars. I should have warned you."

Darn, they know us all too well! Then Bobby walked in, spotted the urinal, and almost had apoplexy. Well, at least we got somebody!

Later, we had more visitors: Mimi, Pop, Jarrod, Erin, and Jose. By then Chris was fairly tired, but he enjoyed the attention. Bobby told them the urinal story, and how he almost had to be resuscitated. We all had a good laugh, and it almost felt like a normal family moment.

We went home on April third. Chris was scheduled to return in ten days for more chemo. He was back in four.

Chris had come home on a Tuesday, and by Friday he told us that he felt his body crashing. He knew his counts were plummeting, and that a fever was inevitable. We knew how disappointed he would be to miss the special weekend at home that we had planned.

We had a lot of my family staying in town, and Chris was anticipating a male-bonding weekend with his favorite uncle, Al. Al is my sister, Maureen's husband, and even though they live in New Jersey, Chris and Al had developed a special relationship over the years. Al frequently called Chris long-distance just to chat. "Why couldn't he be spared a few days to have fun with Al?" I thought angrily.

Saturday, April 7, 2001

... This morning Chris woke up with a 103-degree temperature. We called the answering service, and knowing full well that they'd admit him, we were packed by the time they called us back. So much for our beach weekend with all the family ...

For the next several days Chris spiked very high fevers, and had to be put on morphine for mucositis. He also required transfusions of platelets and packed red cells. Chris handled it with his usual courage and was well enough to go home by Wednesday. But he was expected back at the hospital just a few days after that to begin the second part of his induction.

With Chris's new, uncertain future we decided that I should take a full leave from my job. Fortunately, Bobby's business had grown, and we were in better financial condition than we had been a few years earlier. I was grateful that I could focus entirely on Chris, and our family.

In the meantime our phone was ringing constantly with friends and family members asking us how they could become bone marrow donors. At first, we told them to call the blood bank, but the more we thought about it, we decided that we had an opportunity to reach a lot of people if we had a marrow drive in Chris's honor.

The idea of doing a marrow drive had occurred to us when we first found out that Chris needed a transplant, but the doctors had told us that a local drive would have almost no chance of helping Chris. They had explained that Chris's match would certainly be found on The National Bone Marrow Program's huge international database. Additional computer searches would be done with other, smaller organizations as well. One of them was a cord blood bank.

But the more we talked about it, we realized that all of the samples in those databases came from neighborhood blood drives, from everyday people walking into medical buildings and bloodmobiles and rolling up their sleeves. And we knew that there was always a strong need for units of blood. Having our own blood and marrow drive was the right thing to do.

So organizing the blood drive became my new "job," and my latest mental coping technique. Loaded with nervous energy, freed from the rigors of the classroom, and armed with a cause directly related to my son's survival, I embarked on a mission.

Bob and I began working with the blood bank to set things up, and we learned a lot along the way. For example, getting on the bone marrow registry requires only one small vial of blood. It's actually easier than donating a pint.

If one becomes a bone marrow donor, the procedure is fairly simple—similar to what Chris goes through with his bone marrow aspirations. The patient is sedated, has a needle placed in the bony portion of their lower back or hip, and marrow is extracted from the bone. Usually the donor can go home the same day, and the worst side effect is a tender back for a day or two. And just like donating whole blood, the body replaces the cells in a few weeks. "It's a piece of cake compared to what Chris goes through," I told everyone.

Instead of teaching in the classroom, I would be teaching others how to help save lives. Our greatest hope was that we could save Chris too.

17

THE COMMUNITY REACHES OUT

April 14, 2001

It's been some week, with the family in town, the marrow drive in full swing, and Chris having to go back in again. When we got up here today we noticed a nasty-looking infection on Chris's finger. They called it "cellulitis" and said that they would have to treat it with antibiotics for a few days before starting the chemo—that will mean a longer stay ... Yesterday Chris's hair started falling out again. It had barely just grown back. Bobby took him to a local barber to get it shaved. They were very nice, and let him come in after closing and didn't charge him ...

The next day was Easter Sunday—an Easter I will never forget. Father John, our parish priest, came up to the hospital and celebrated Easter Mass for us in Chris's hospital room. (We all love Father John, who manages to be young, humorous, and wise all at the same time.) It was just the five of us and my parents, praying intimately together, with Father John delivering our own special sermon of healing and hope.

Later that evening the doctors gave Chris a two-hour pass to go out with us. Since his infection had delayed the start of the chemo, and his antibiotics were now done, they allowed us to take him out to dinner. For a blissful hour or so all that we had to worry about was bad food and lousy service.

The following day we got some preliminary results from the bone marrow searches.

April 16, 2001

I met with Paula (the bone marrow nurse). She reported that some promising samples had arrived. There were two possible adult matches and two possible cord blood matches. They are only "possible" matches because further genetic level testing must be done on the samples to see if they are suitable for Chris. I learned that it's a very com-

plicated process with many variables including which cell groups match and how con-
centrated the volume of stem cells is. I can see why this process is expensive. But how do
you put a price on saving a life?

Two days later a local news channel came up to the hospital to do a story about Chris. They spent over an hour with Chris and interviewed both him and Bobby. (I was at home with Erin and Jarrod.) As I watched Chris on the news that evening, I was struck by his poise and dignity. He wasn't a scared little boy any more. I watched a courageous young man speak calmly of better days ahead. "I'm looking forward to getting better and going to school and playing soccer," he said. Then the cameraman zoomed in on his freckles.

The news story helped to rally the community around us, and it generated publicity for our upcoming blood and marrow drive, which was just a few days away. It was comforting to know that our whole city was praying for us.

The day before Chris went home The Tampa Bay Buccaneers came up to 2 Southwest to visit all of the patients. Offensive lineman Jerry Wunsch told Chris about a special camp that he offered for young cancer patients each February. Jerry and his wife take a group up to Wisconsin every year for winter sports. "That's how my wife and I celebrate our anniversary," he explained.

"What a wonderful way to celebrate your anniversary—by helping those kids!" I had responded with tears in my eyes. They weren't just tears of gratitude—they were tears of longing—hoping that Chris would survive until next February to enjoy the camp.

I will always remember April 22, 2001, as the day Sarasota hugged us. The blood and bone marrow drive set a new record at The Suncoast Community Blood Bank for both units of blood and bone marrow samples collected in one day.

Besides the publicity from the news report we had recruited family and friends to distribute flyers all over town. There is no better way to get anything accomplished than to assign it to a small army of teachers who are used to doing five things at once anyway. Within days the town was plastered with Chris's picture, and we had a list of volunteers for the event.

But knowing all of that, we still weren't prepared for the crowd that showed up. Even with three bloodmobiles the lines stretched around the parking lot, and the wait was over two hours. No one complained, and we received countless hugs.

Our local supermarket, Publix, provided huge trays of food to feed the volunteers, and when the bloodmobiles ran out of ice and orange juice they provided that as well. When the volunteers ran out of donation forms, the store manager gave us his office and copier to use for the day. Our parents and aunts and uncles were kept busy all day copying and collating the three-page forms, scrambling to meet the demand. Another supermarket across the street sent food over, also. I imagine that that was the first time in history a supermarket actually sent food to its competitor!

Chris was at home and was able to attend for brief periods of time. Our home was just around the corner from the shopping center, so we assigned shuttle duty to Erin. She would go get Chris, who would stay until he was tired, then she would run him home.

In the meantime news crews from two stations showed up to interview us and get shots of the crowd. Chris was outgoing and cheerful on camera, and I realized what a hero he had become. When the news crews left Chris went home, exhausted, and took a nap.

Looking back on that day, I realize that many gifts were given. First was the gift of life. Hundreds of much-needed units of blood were added to the area supply, and many new marrow registrants were added to the registry. Second was the gift of awareness. At the drive countless people came up to me and said, "I had no idea there was such a need," or "I didn't know it was this easy to donate (or be typed as a marrow donor)."

Our greatest hope that day was that we would be given the gift of a new lease on life for Chris, but even though we knew that those chances were slim, we received a gift that I will cherish forever. Seeing a whole town come together in an act of love on our behalf renewed our faith in man and in God.

And that coming together, I think, was the final gift that day. Chris had given our neighbors an opportunity to make a difference, to show love, to be heroes. People get so caught up in their busy lives, going to work, chauffeuring their kids to school and sports, wondering what to fix for dinner, that they just don't get that opportunity. We can't all be policemen, fireman, or war heros, but I think we've all wished would could save someone. So for one beautiful day in Sarasota we all tried.

Chris had another scheduled chemo admit on May 8. By then the doctors had had the chance to further study the marrow samples, and they planned to meet with us that week to update us. In preparation for transplant they ordered tests of his heart and lung function.

May 9, 2001 (Bob's entry)

... We are getting down to the nitty-gritty now. I'm starting to get really nervous. We have done all that we can for Chris. Now it's in God's hands ... 10:30 AM—Chris had an EKG. 11:00 AM—the hospital dietitian visited and went over Chris's diet for post transplantation. Kim from child-life visited to tell us about life in isolation, and the activities that they have to offer. This afternoon Chris will have an ultrasound. The doctors seem to agree that they want to do a cord blood transplant on Chris. His bone marrow transplant admission date is May 29. First he will have surgery to have a Broviac (another catheter used for infusing meds and blood products) installed near his port. This is where the new bone marrow will be introduced into his body ... Whoever was in room 274 died last night. lots of crying people and clergy around ...

After Chris's latest relapse, he began to speak more of Heaven and his angels. He often mentioned his friends, Robert and Jo Jo. Sometimes he described what he thought they were doing in Heaven, and other times he asked me what I thought they were doing. We discussed the fact that they were spirits without solid bodies, and how fun and exhilarating that must be. I imagined that the feeling of love they felt all the time must be a hundred times greater than the love we experienced at the bone marrow drive.

We both agreed that Heaven must be too awesome for us to even imagine. "For us to try to understand what Heaven's like is probably like trying to teach algebra to a dog," I had commented.

But Chris had realized something that takes most adult a lifetime to grasp: Death is a natural part of living, and it's perfectly OK to talk about it. And death isn't necessarily a bad thing—it's a transition to a greater existence. With each successive setback, the possibility of death was looming closer. Chris was reaching out to understand, rather than avoid, the issue. We encouraged to him to explore and admired him for his courage.

By speaking so openly Chris was also, wisely, eliminating his own fear. He had come to the conclusion that death wasn't anything to be afraid of, no matter how old or young you were. Besides, he had his own personal guardian angels waiting for him. However, regardless of how attractive Heaven was, Chris wasn't about to give up his fight to live.

May 10, 2001

Chris had a hearing test this morning—more double-checking to make sure that there is no chemo damage. Bobby and I couldn't go because we were meeting with Paula, the transplant nurse.

Paula spent a good hour with us explaining things and answering our questions. We learned that the matching process begins with analyzing proteins on the surface of the cells called "antigens." There are six antigens, so of course the most desirable match is six out of six, but achieving a match that close is extremely rare. Transplants can be done with five out of six and four out of six as long as certain other genetic factors are compatible. They had found some five out of six adult matches and some four out of six cord matches for Chris.

Surprisingly, Dr. Rossbach had chosen one of the four out of six cord matches as the best option for Chris. Paula explained that the greater mismatch in the cord blood didn't matter nearly as much as it would have in an adult sample. The cord blood is so new it changes and adapts. Also, there is a significantly lower risk of rejection with cord blood. The cord donor they have chosen has a good cell count—enough volume for someone Chris's size.

Paula gave us the schedule. This is Chris's last chemo admit, then he'll have two and a half weeks at home. He'll be admitted on the twenty-ninth to have the Broviac put in. This will be followed by four days of total body radiation, then two days of a drug called "cytoxam" (God, that even sounds toxic!). Then the actual transplant will be on June 6. That's the day before Erin graduates from high school ...

When we got back to Chris's room we asked him how his hearing test went, and he said, "What?"

I remembered the many times that I had spoken with the parents of bone marrow kids, and how awful the process seemed. Now here we were facing it. After almost four years of treatment, and more than two years of remission, we had never thought it would come to this.

But at the same time, it was also a new lease on life. Chris would be getting a brand-new immune system. Maybe that's what he had needed all along to finally kill the enemy within.

As had been the case so many times before, Chris didn't get to stay home during his time off. Just four days after coming home I found myself racing up the interstate toward the hospital, with Chris lying in the back of my van, groaning in pain and clutching his back. I considered calling an ambulance, but we had done that once before, and since it was across county lines and past several closer hospitals, there had been a wait time for the dispatcher to relay permission. I knew I would be faster.

It took a couple of days for them to figure out what the problem was, and thank God, it wasn't cancer. Chris had had so many spinals and bone marrow aspirations that he had tissue swelling compressing his spine. They also suspected that he was having muscle spasms in his back. They put him on an antiseizure medicine called neurontin. It also works as a muscle relaxant that blocks pain signals. After going on the neurontin Chris improved quickly.

In the meantime, we had waged one final battle regarding pain management. The previous admit, Chris's back had been hurting as well. Bobby had gone to bed at the RMH, and Chris had called to complain. He told Bobby his back was really hurting and the only thing they were giving him was tylenol. Bobby had marched over and raised hell. "Who cares if he's addicted to pain meds? This is the least of our worries. I want him made comfortable!"

After that, the doctors had finally agreed that Chris's requests for pain medication would no longer be questioned. This lifted a huge burden off of our shoulders as well as Chris's. I am certain that they had no clue what a huge source of stress that had been for us. Only someone who has seen their child suffer needlessly could possibly understand.

We had other mental burdens as well. As parents of such a seriously ill child we sometimes questioned whether or not we were doing the right thing. So, during the previous few weeks I had also called a few major cancer centers around the country. I had Chris's files sent to a well-known leukemia expert, and I spoke with him on the phone. He told me what I wanted to hear: that he would use the exact same treatment that Chris was receiving at All Children's. We needed to be reassured that we were doing everything that we could, and that Chris was receiving the best care possible.

On the bright side, Chris received a call from another local wish organization, The Kids Wish Network. The Kids Wish Network, unlike most such organizations, grants second wishes to children who have relapsed, or whose condition has worsened. The timing was perfect. Chris desperately needed something special to look forward to.

Chris chose a shopping spree at Toys R Us. This was a good, practical decision since he could stock up on games and activities to keep himself occupied during his upcoming isolation.

The Kids Wish Network did an outstanding job. They had to throw things together rather quickly since Chris's transplant was rapidly approaching. We also lucked out because Chris's counts were acceptable to go out in public that day.

We were picked up by limousine, and treated like VIPs. An added bonus was the fact that our shopping partners were Cara and Aaron Stecker. Cara works for The Kids Wish Network, and when she heard that we were Tampa Bay fans she brought along her husband, Aaron, a Bucs running back. I joked to Bob, who has had season tickets to the Bucs since 1976, that he was getting his wish, too.

Once again, we had been the recipients of a great act of kindness. I don't even pretend to understand why our kind and clever Christopher has had to suffer so much, but I continue to be awed by the outpouring of love that has been channeled our way.

Another place where Chris knew that he could absorb large quantities of love and affection was at Bay Haven. During his remaining days at home Chris enjoyed visiting the school, and chatting with his former teachers.

The gals in the office would let Chris use the intercom system to send out his greetings. Miss Keil, his fifth-grade teacher and homebound tutor, was an avid collector of pig paraphernalia. Her room was filled with pig posters, stuffed pigs, and ceramic pigs. So when Chris hailed her over the PA he always said, "How are all the little piggies doing?"

Of course, we couldn't resist pestering my class, which was being taught by my partner, Laurie. Chris would push the PA button, and in a deep-throated voice bellow, "Wasssup!" (a popular slang expression for "what's up?"). All of us in the office would chuckle as we heard the commotion on the other side.

The last few times Chris and I visited before his scheduled transplant we had informed Barbara, the registrar, that Chris was getting cord blood that would most likely come from The New York Placental Bank. Barbara, or "Babs" as we all call her, is a pure-bred lasagna-cooking New York Italian. "Chris!" She exclaimed, "You're gett'in that good New Yawk blood! Now listen kid, you gotta practice saying, 'YO MA!' And you gotta do the hand gesture like this, see," and Babs would demonstrate the appropriate, sweeping arm movement.

So, after that, every time Chris came with me to pick up Jarrod at school, he'd stick his head in the office and yell, "YO MA!"

On May 29 Chris went into the short-stay surgical unit and had his Broviac catheter inserted. Chris wasn't looking forward to this new addition to his endless list of inconveniences. Unlike the mediport, which isn't visible when it's not being used, the Broviac tubing hangs from an incision in the chest.

The surgical unit was swamped, which made for a long, tiring day. There was a lot of waiting around, and Chris was weak and tired from fasting. In addition, he had developed a cough, so we also had to wait for chest and sinus x-rays to determine if Chris was healthy enough for the surgery.

They went ahead with the surgery, but decided to delay the radiation, which was supposed to begin the following day. Chris had bronchitis. This meant Chris could go home for a few days, so he was thrilled. I had a bad feeling.

May 29, 2001

… Always before, we'd celebrated the chance to go home, but I just don't feel that way now. I want to get on with this. I hate this waiting … I asked Dr. Rossbach if he thought Chris was in danger of relapsing again, and he said, "no." Then why am I so afraid to take him home?

18

DEVASTATION

Chris was due back in the clinic the following Monday for more tests, and to see if he had recovered enough to start his radiation. That day we began yet another nightmare.

June 4, 2001

... Dr. Grana looked at his blood smears under a microscope, and didn't like what she saw. This was followed by a bone marrow aspiration, confirming our worst fears. There's leukemia in the marrow! WHY DOESN'T CHRIS EVER GET A BREAK?

They can't go ahead with the transplant unless Chris is in remission ... The plan: another cycle of chemo with new drugs—hoping to knock him back into remission. Then do the transplant. This is our last chance. More fear. More delays. More nail biting ...

This was the most devastating news we had ever had. It was Chris's third relapse. His odds for survival were miniscule. All we could do was pray for a miracle.

My emotions ran the gamut from shock to anger to fear, and I imagined that Chris's did also. But he had one additional one we hadn't expected: relief. "Mom," he said, "I was really scared of that radiation. I'm more afraid of that than the bone marrow transplant." He didn't mind the fact that his radiation would be postponed.

But Bob and I did. The transplant schedule had been our final plan of attack, the all-out assault with our biggest weapons, our only remaining weapons. We had worked hard mentally to prepare ourselves for this. The car was packed for a summer in the hospital and we had given Chris pep talks about how he would receive brand-new cancer-free marrow.

Now the rug had been snatched out from under us. We were given two choices: Take him home and enjoy the time that he has left, or one more cycle of chemo—a last ditch effort to attain remission. They would try different drugs.

Of course, Bob and my first reaction was, "We have to try!" but we also realized that Chris had to make the final decision. We would not force him to submit to more chemotherapy if he wasn't willing.

So, in one of the hardest conversations parents could ever have with a beloved child, we discussed the options. We were tearful, but managed to remain calm. When we were done talking Chris said, "I won't give up."

June 5, 2001

*Dr. Rossbach went over Chris's treatment plan with us. He'll start the chemo today. He said that these are very big drugs, and Chris may require three or four weeks to recover. What a blow—another month of being in limbo. How are we going to stand it? What are we going to do to keep from getting depressed and going crazy? Before there was always a plan. We had the drug protocol, and then the expected results. Now the rules of the game have all changed ... Now **we** are one of those less fortunate families that I used to feel sorry for.*

I won't give up. I won't stop fighting. Don't quit Chris. We're with you ...

That first day Chris had a spinal that went badly. They either hit a nerve or Chris had a muscle spasm in his back. They had to give him some morphine. Was this a sign of what was yet to come?

But if we'd had any doubts about Chris being able to muster his usual courage and spirit after this latest blow, they were soon laid to rest. Later that day, after Chris had recovered from the disastrous spinal, Kim from child-life came by with a special gift. Months earlier she had told us about an organization called "The Songs of Love Foundation." It's a nonprofit music company that writes and records original personalized songs for seriously ill children. Kim had helped Chris fill out a biographical form, and they had sent it away to New York to have Chris's own CD made. We had completely forgotten about it until Kim brought it up to Chris's room.

Just as Kim was about to play the song for us, Miss Lucy, the transport nurse, came to get Chris for an x-ray. Lucy was one of my favorite hospital characters. She was an elderly black woman who'd worked at the hospital since its inception as a children's hospital back in the mid-sixties. (Chris and I called her "Lucy In The Sky with Diamonds" because she once told us that she was the longest standing employee. When I suggested that they buy her a gold watch, she had said, "No, honey, I want diamonds!") So when Chris asked her if he could bring his boom box to radiology we knew she'd say "sure."

June 5, 2001 cont'd

... so we went down to radiology with a boom box and listened to "Chris's Rap." Chris got up out of his wheelchair and grooved around the room with Lucy while the radiology technicians laughed ...

> *THERE'S ONLY ONE THING ON MY WISH LIST*
> *TO SPEND SOME TIME WITH CHRIS*
> *LISTEN CLOSE I'M GONNA TELL YOU THIS*
> *THERE'S NO ONE IN THE WORLD QUITE LIKE CHRIS*
> *CHRIS DITMARS YEA HE'S THE MAN ...*

So there was my boy, facing the fear of death, and he had us all rapping in radiology. Chris had answered my question about how we were going to keep from going crazy. He was just going to continue to be his same, amazing self.

June 6, 2001

Today's the day they would have done the transplant ... Bobby's been busy getting things ready at home—cleaning, painting, new carpet being put in. (When a local company had heard of our situation they had donated all new carpet for our home.) *Bobby even washed all of the stuffed animals in Chris's room. I would have just gotten rid of them. It makes me smile to picture the little critters bouncing around in our washer and dryer ... Please God, let us make it to transplant ...*

The following day they had to redo the botched spinal. It was a necessary procedure to check the spinal fluid for cancer and to inject chemotherapy. Chris had been in so much pain the other day that they hadn't been able to complete the procedure. This time we insisted that he be given general anesthesia, and it went much better. That was also the day that Erin graduated from high school.

June 7, 2001

... Today Chris is looking at me with angry eyes instead of the loving ones that I'm used to. I can't blame him. Nothing I've promised him has come true. We just keep getting bad news on top of bad news ... I hate to leave him alone to go to Erin's graduation ...

I felt like we had let Erin down too. So much of her teen years had been overshadowed by Chris's treatments, and now her graduation night was also. Under the circumstances we couldn't have a party or celebrate properly. "Don't worry, Mom and Dad," she said, trying to make us feel better, "I have lots of parties to go to."

Instead of feeling happy that night I was sad, thinking that we were launching her into the world after four years of neglecting her. Once again, I forced my brain to think positive thoughts. "You have two children about to begin a whole new life," I said to myself. Then added in a whisper, "Did you hear that, God?"

June 8, 2001

... It's Friday and Chris hasn't eaten since Tuesday. It's so hard seeing him like this—no Silly String, no blonde jokes for Nancy, no bumper pool. I'm so lonely. Most of my friends have stopped calling.

... Finally about 10:00 PM Chris perked up and I saw a little bit of playfulness return. He coughed into his bucket and asked the nurse to come in and "admire" it. That just shows that it's the sickness form the chemo that's got him down, not his mental outlook, because he's back to his old tricks as soon as he feels a little bit better. He's my hero.

Besides Erin's graduation we had our anniversary, Chris's birthday, and Bob's birthday all in one week, but all we could focus on was Chris. The new drugs were making Chris very nauseous, and he was only able to be his normal humorous self for very short periods of time.

His fourteenth birthday was on the tenth, and he spent a large part of it vomiting. The nurses made a banner, and brought in a cake that Chris could barely stand to look at. He did perk up a bit when they brought in his gift—a remote control jeep. He was able to sit up for a while and play with it, but even that little bit of activity tired him out.

As I sat by his bed watching his exhausted sleep I thought about previous birthdays—days of sunshine and pool parties. I remembered his first birthday when he sat in his high chair, playfully slapping his hands on the tray, his cheeks and silky blonde hair covered in chocolate cake. I remembered his fifth birthday when he was trying out his bike without training wheels for the very first time. He hopped on fearlessly and took off wobbling down the street. He had no idea how to stop so he deliberately ran into a mailbox, and leaped aside laughing as the bicycle tumbled to the ground. I remembered his twelfth birthday, when he had been in remission for more than a year. He had romped with his cousins and sprayed the air with his water gun. More scenes from happier times flashed through my mind, and I looked at my son and cried.

June 10, 2001

Happy birthday, Chris! We love you so much. You're going to beat this. You're going to be our miracle boy.

Early this morning I ran with Mati and some other nurses. They listened with kindness and sympathy while I poured my heart out. It was like a moving prayer group. Will God hear me better if I'm out of breath?

... Jane and Kevin Wilson stopped by. (Kevin was Chris's very first roommate, and we've seen them a lot over the years. He's in remission and doing well.) I visited with them in the hall because Chris wasn't feeling well. Kevin looks great. He has a good head of hair. He's gained weight and he's taller. Part of me thinks that maybe I should hate their guts. Maybe it's a sign that God is with me because I don't.

After Chris's transplant, when we finally get the word that his new marrow has grafted, I'm going to carry a big sign to tell the whole world while I roller-blade up and down the halls.

I had never seen Chris more nauseous than he was for the next several days. They were giving him the largest possible doses of chemo that a human body could survive. Once again, I wondered if there were some things worse than death.

I performed mental gymnastics in order to stay positive. I sought out magazine stories with quotes like "They only gave me 3 months to live, and now here I am, three years later ..." When Chris was well enough to talk he continued to say that he wouldn't give up. Neither would I.

June 11, 2001

... Thought of the week: The bronchitis delay was a good thing because it gave them a chance to detect his relapse, which they might have missed had they proceeded with the transplant. Without this additional chemo his transplant wouldn't have been successful. Now it will be!

A few days later after Chris was stabilized we were sent home to wait—wait for his counts to bottom out, wait for them to come back up, and wait for the results of one final bone marrow aspiration to see if the chemo worked.

As usual, a fever robbed Chris of most of his time at home. A few short days after going home his temperature started to creep up. Like trained military strategists, Bob and I mapped out our schedules for the week, but we also made a decision that we knew wouldn't sit well with Chris. We felt that he couldn't afford any more delays, so we decided to keep him in the hospital until transplant.

June 18, 2001

Chris's temperature started going up yesterday. We arrived this morning about 4:30 AM with Chris spiking as high as 104.4. Tylenol brought it back down. Counts are very low. Chris will need transfusions of platelets and a couple of units of red blood.

This is it—the final round. We are living the cliché "Do or Die."

Chris tested positive for strep as well as a stool bacterium that had gotten into his blood. When counts are low bacteria that normally remain in the intestines can migrate into the blood. This was scary—we had seen several cancer patients with low counts die from opportunistic infections. The doctors agreed with us that it was a good idea to keep Chris hospitalized for the remainder of his treatments.

None of this seemed to faze Chris for long. The antibiotics and the ativan (the drug used for nausea and anxiety) were making him comfortable, so he was free to be his free-wheeling self for a while.

June 19, 2001

… Chris was quite lively this afternoon. When Grandmommy called he disguised his voice and he had her convinced that she had the wrong number, but he fessed up just as she was about to hang up. I cringed and laughed at the same time when I listened to the rest of the conversation. "Grandmommy, I like your cooking a lot better than Aunt Lisa's." There was a pause while I assumed that my mom was responding to the compliment. Then Chris continued, "She sent over a casserole the other night and it gave us all diarrhea." I laughed so hard that I almost fell out of my chair.

Chris also spoke with Uncle Al on the phone and that conversation consisted largely of reminiscing about a time that they had gone out for burgers and Chris had laughed so hard that French fries had come out of his nose.

I remember listening and thinking that that was the kind of conversation that adolescent boys should have—gross and disgusting. Chris had missed those opportunities for lunchroom antics and teenage hallway banter—the goofy stuff most kids his age take for granted.

However, Chris didn't stop having the serious and spiritual conversations either.

June 19, 2001

… We talked a lot about souls and Heaven today. Chris said that he thinks Heaven has a section just for kids. "There's a giant soda bar," he explained, "not just your regular flavors like cherry and coke, but every single flavor that was ever invented, plus

some that haven't been invented—all different colors." His theory was that even though the souls didn't have bodies they could still enjoy their favorite sensations from Earth.

"There's dogs in Heaven too," he continued. "Remember how Moonshine always used to drop the Frisbee when we threw it to him? Well, Jo Jo and Robert have taught him how to catch it! He's leaping up over the clouds catching it and floating around."

Chris also said he had a good feeling about getting better and growing up. He felt that God wanted him to become a child-life specialist at a hospital. "I will know exactly how those kids feel."

Hearing Chris talk about his future like that almost made it all make sense. For him to grow up and convert his years of suffering into a way to help other children would be my ultimate dream come true. It would give a meaning and a purpose to the last four years.

I tried to imagine Chris, tall and grown up, striding down these same hospital corridors, visiting all of the patients, entertaining them and comforting them. What a perfect job for him. I could picture the scenario, but I had trouble picturing Chris as a healthy adult.

June 21, 2001

I had a good run this morning. I usually do when I know that Chris is resting comfortably. When I got up to the room I just watched him sleep. I love him so much it hurts.

> *Pray pray, every day,*
> *Cancer cancer, go away.*
> *Let Chris have some time to play,*
> *Let him grow up someday.*
> *Pray pray, every day.*

Chris was handling the waiting game well. His counts were still too low for the doctors to test his bone marrow for remission. Dr. Rossbach said that Chris was responding well to the antibiotics, and he was hoping he'd be ready in about two weeks. In the meantime Chris did low-level activities like watching movies, playing poker, and letting Gail, the teacher, read to him. He was fond of Gary Paulsen novels. Paulsen writes survival stories about a young man Chris's age who becomes trapped in the wilderness and must fend for himself. Very appropriate reading material, I thought. Again, I was amazed at Chris's ability to find his own therapeutic outlets.

Good old Nurse Nancy was still a therapeutic outlet as well. One day when she passed by Chris shot some jokes at her, "Hey, Smelly Melly, if a blonde and a brunette fall off a cliff do you know who hits first?"

"I don't want to know, I have work to do," she answered, trying to sound angry.

"The brunette hits first, because the blonde has to stop and ask directions!" By then Nancy was half way down the hall, but we knew that she had heard us.

A week later his counts weren't any better, and by then, we were all emotionally frazzled. Waiting for the counts to rise enough to do the bone marrow aspiration was the equivalent of waiting to find out if Chris was going to live or die. It was like living a moment of terror in slow motion, like a crime victim who has a gun pointed at his head. "Is the perpetrator going to pull the trigger or let me go?" the terrified victim asks himself. That gut-wrenching moment dragged on for days.

Then the wait was over.

June 28, 2001

Today they ran a CBC (complete blood count) and I asked for a copy of it. IT SHOWED BLASTS. Dr. Rossbach was still on rounds and hadn't seen it yet. I cornered him in the hall and showed it to him. "That's not good," he said.

As a result, he decided to go ahead and do the bone marrow aspiration today. I paced and cried, and Bobby and I prayed with Chaplain Paul.

I didn't want Chris to see how scared I was, but he did. He actually reassured me and told me that he's a survivor ...

... Oh God, it was the worst news possible. The chemo didn't work. IT DIDN'T WORK. The blasts are leukemia and they are sending him home to die. Our fourteen-year-old son is being sent home to die.

19

CHRIS'S GOLDEN HOURS

The next few days were really a lifetime. It was a lifetime because we had to face the abrupt end of one. It was a lifetime because we had to try to express a lifetime of thoughts. It was a lifetime because we felt a lifetime of emotions.

Chris already knew even before Dr. Rossbach came into his room and asked to speak to Bob and me. We asked the doctor to take us to a private room, and we told Chris that we'd be right back. Dr. Rossbach told us what we already knew, that there was no hope.

Chris didn't wait for us to send for him. He walked in a few minutes later. We shouldn't have left him behind. He was crying and saying, "I'm going to die." Then he sat on the sofa between Bob and me, and we all embraced. I'm not sure how long the three of us sat like that, hugging each other and saying over and over again, "I love you." Maybe it was twenty minutes; maybe it was a lifetime.

"I'm going to be your guardian angel," Chris declared through his tears, "And I'm going to ask Jesus to let me appear to you."

After we all sat alone for a while, Chris asked us to bring the doctor back in so he could ask him some questions.

June 28, 2001 cont'd

Chris: Will I be in pain?
Dr. Rossbach: No, we'll give you all the medicine you need to be pain-free.
Chris: How long do you think I have?
Dr. R: It's hard to say. Weeks, maybe months.
Chris: Can I get my Broviac out so I can swim in my pool?
Dr. R: Yes.
Chris: Will I die in my sleep?
Dr. R: Probably.

The following day was the most memorable day in my life. Chris somehow managed to live his own version of his golden years all in one afternoon. All day long he had amazing and profound conversations with us and with the staff.

June 29, 2001

... Dr. Rossbach came in and sat on Chris's bed for a long time telling him angel stories, stories about other children he's known who have died. Many of them had vivid and inspiring dreams about Heaven. Some of them were clinically dead, then came back long enough to say that they had met their angels. My favorite story was the "Abigail" story. It goes like this: A woman had a child who died of leukemia, but before she died the little girl told her that she had a dream about a beautiful angel named Abigail who comforted her and told her about Heaven. The little girl died shortly afterward, and the mother remained a bit puzzled about the identity of her daughter's angel since she had never known anyone named Abigail. A few months later, she was sitting on a park bench and started a conversation with another woman sitting next to her. To her amazement, she soon discovered that this woman had also lost a daughter to leukemia. That woman's daughter had died not long before her own child. Her name was Abigail.

As Dr. Rossbach told that story I noticed tears in his eyes. It was the first time I had ever seen him cry. It comforted me to know that he cared.

All day long nurses and staff members approached Bob and me to pay tribute to Chris, and to tell us how at peace he seemed. Several of them took us aside and said, "We didn't tell you this sooner, but Chris said good-bye to us last week. He thanked us and he told us that he loved us."

"Last week!" Bobby and I had repeated to ourselves. It was only yesterday that we had been told that Chris was terminal. I cried and let my emotions wash over me. It was time to surrender to a higher power. Chris had probably started making his peace long before we realized. He must already be in touch with angels.

Chris's conversation with Nurse Jem was the best of all. Jemma was what Chris referred to as a "fox."

June 29, 2001 cont'd

... "Jemma," Chris said, "when I die you are going to be so heartbroken that you'll want to kill yourself. It will be just like Romeo and Juliet. So I think that you should hurry up and marry me before it's too late." Jemna smiled and agreed that she would start referring to Chris as her "husband." Chris's new name for her would be "babe." After that Jem started calling me "mom" ...

I laughed and cried at the same time. Only Chris could find the humor and the irony in the fact that he would never marry, never present me with a sweet young women to call me "Mom" and bear our grandchildren.

Chris had connected with each nurse in a unique and special way, and he was saying good-bye to each in the same individual way.

Petite little Maria, the same nurse that we had victimized on April Fool's Day with the colored urine, was there that week also. Dark-haired and doe-eyed, she moved in and out of the room almost noiselessly, taking pains not to disturb Chris when he was sleeping. Chris called her "the reindeer," and it suited her. Not long beforehand Chris had found out that she was from Miami. So every time she came into the room Chris made her dance a few steps and sing a few bars from the song "Welcome to Miami."

The patients had all decided that cute, bubbly Denise resembled a "Smurf" cartoon character when she donned the plastic blue gowns that the nurses were required to wear when hanging chemo. So that last time Chris saw her he simply said, "Bye, Smurf, I love you."

Tall, blonde Victoria from Canada had been Chris's Nintendo buddy during the months that she had worked the night shift. While the floor was quiet, and everyone else was sleeping Victoria had played video games with Chris in the wee hours of the morning. Chris had enjoyed teasing her about her Canadian accent and her ugly orange suede sneakers. He told her that he wanted her to wrap them up and give them to Nurse Nancy for Christmas.

But it was when I returned from a short break, thinking that Chris was asleep, that I saw him in all of his glory. He was holding court at the nurses' station, seated in one of the rolling office chairs, surrounded by Nancy and the others. They were all laughing and playing an electronic trivia game. Chris was telling Nancy that she wouldn't know any of the answers because she was blonde. So I sat down with them and lived in the moment. It was the most beautiful moment of my life. As I glanced around I noticed that Chris had changed the screen saver on their computer so that it scrolled the words "Chris loves Jemma."

I think almost anyone who has lived to middle age or beyond can recall some personal days of glory, whether it is making a game-winning touchdown on the high school grid iron, watching the birth of your child, getting that big promotion, or proudly escorting your children around in their homemade Halloween costumes. It's those days of our lives when we can look back and say, "I made a difference. I achieved something."

I believe that Friday afternoon in June was a great day of glory for Chris. Instead of retreating in sorrow he connected with everyone as if to say, "I love you all, and I am loved. I am Chris. Remember me."

At approximately 3:30 PM Chris's golden hours ended. That was when the pain began. It started with a reaction from an infusion of platelets that left Chris shivering and wincing in pain. He complained of severe leg pain, and after two infusions of morphine he still wasn't comfortable, so they put him on a continuous drip with a PCA button. (It allowed him to self-administer a safe amount of morphine.)

Before Chris's pain crisis we had been told that we could take him home the next day, but now that was looking doubtful. First, we would have to get his pain under control, and then figure out a way to manage it at home.

Finally, after what seemed like forever, Chris was comfortable enough to talk.

June 29, 2001 cont'd

... While I was back at RMH packing Bobby and Chris were talking about when Chris goes to Heaven. Bobby had asked Chris if he would send a sign or a signal to us after he dies. "So that I know you're OK," he had said.

"What would you like?" Chris had asked.

"A feather," Bobby had responded, "how about leaving a feather under my pillow?"

"OK, Dad, I'll see what I can do," Chris had replied.

As I listened to Bobby recount the conversation I realized that it was almost as if Bobby and Chris had reversed roles. Now Chris was the father, and Bobby was the son ...

In the space of less than twenty-four hours our priorities had completely changed. We had gone from trying to save our son's life to just wanting to bring him home to die. We had discussed our options well. The doctors had left it up to us, and Chris had been adamant that he die in his own home. He would go home to Hospice care.

Just to be sure we also asked him if he wanted to try chemo one more time, but he said "No, no more chemo."

I had grown to trust Chris's instincts. He knew that he was dying, and we had to accept it. I thought about all the times he had been right in the past. He could always tell when he was getting ready to spike a fever, when his counts were dropping, and he had known that he'd relapsed before anyone told him. So now I trusted him that no more chemo was the right choice.

While the past four years had been so very difficult, I was grateful for the open, loving relationship that we had shared with Chris. I was glad that I had recorded so much in my journal. That is what gave me the idea to have others share as well.

I went to a local drugstore and bought a composition book. My plan was to pass it around to the staff at the hospital and invite anyone who cared to, to write about Chris. On the first page I wrote the following letter:

Dear Friends at All Children's,

Please take a few moments to write down your thoughts or memories about our beloved Chris. If you recall a conversation or a shared experience together, tell us about it.

Chris spent a large portion of his childhood here at All Children's, and I think, has literally grown up here. In many ways he's been our teacher, enduring his treatments with a dignity and sense of humor far beyond his years.

Thank you all for the love and support that you've given us. We will never forget you, as we know you won't forget our Chris.

Love,
The Ditmars
Maribeth, Bob, Chris, Erin and Jarrod

June 30, 2001

Today is the fourth anniversary of Chris's first diagnosis. We had so much hope then. What a long, weary, road we have traveled. I never thought that it would end up like this.

Chris required an increase in morphine last night and again this morning. Dr. Rossbach recommended that we keep Chris here until Monday because Hospice won't be able to get everything arranged properly until then.

We had a lot of company today. There were all of us, my parents, Pat, Donna, Justin, and Andrew. (My brother, Pat, who lives in Pennsylvania, brought his family down.) Chris could only tolerate a short visit, then I went down to the cafeteria with Pat, Donna, and the kids while Bobby and Erin stayed with Chris. I watched Justin and Jarrod scamper around the cafeteria (Justin is a few years younger than Chris) while I sat with Pat and Donna. Baby Andrew cooed happily in his stroller. It makes me ache with sadness to realize that he'll never know Chris.

Back in the room after everyone else left, Erin got up to leave also. But as soon as she was gone Chris asked me to bring her back. I dashed outside and caught her. They talked quietly for a while, nice, normal small talk, and then Chris gently fell asleep. He had wanted one last visit alone with his sister.

... We had to tell Jarrod today that Chris was dying. We took him up to our room at RMH, good old room, 35, our home away from home. Jarrod sat in the rocker with tears in his eyes while we explained that his big brother was going to Heaven. He sat still for a moment, and just let his glasses fall off of his face. After a minute or two he started asking questions. With his seven-year-old logic Jarrod compared what will happen to Chris with the death of Moonshine.

We assured Jarrod that there was nothing for him to catch or to be afraid of. We tried to be positive, telling him that Chris would be our guardian angel.

Chris continued to require hourly increases in his morphine. The cancer was taking over his body. The nurses reported that his respirations were dropping when he was asleep, but they were OK when he was awake. He had brief periods when he was his old self again. He got up to pee in his urinal bucket, and asked me to close the curtain and guard the door. "If Jem came by and saw me there could be big trouble."

He also managed to tease me. When I misunderstood something Bobby said Chris remarked, "Mom, you were a blonde in another life."

Then, just like that, he was back in pain again. There was no upper limit to his morphine dose, but he wasn't allowed to increase more than one milligram per hour. He could also hit the PCA button.

July 1, 2001

... I asked Chris if he wanted me to hit his PCA button for him, but he said, "No, Mom, I'm a big boy. I have opposable thumbs." I laughed in spite of myself, in spite of the horrendous situation. Chris is giving joy and humor to the very end ...

By that afternoon we knew that the morphine alone wasn't controlling Chris's continuously increasing pain. So they hooked up another pump, an anesthesia drug called ketamine.

More visitors arrived, this time Bobby's side of the family. All of Chris's cousins were coming to say good-bye. I thought of all of the large family gatherings that we had enjoyed over the years, the birthdays, holidays, and family parties. Chris would no longer be a part of that. Our family landscape would be changed forever. I couldn't imagine it without our Chris.

Father Gerry, our pastor came also. He brought communion and performed the anointing of the sick. I told Father Gerry that I think I know how the Blessed Mother felt when she saw her son hanging on the cross.

July 1, 2001 cont'd

Chris didn't mind the activity. He told us to just sit around him and have regular conversations, so that's what we did. Chris drifted in and out of consciousness, but I think he heard more than it appeared he did. I think he was comforted by the buzz of familiar voices. They were like an audible blanket of love surrounding him.

The following day Chris was reporting less pain. Adding the ketamine seemed to help a lot, but it also gave Chris some double vision and made him a little less coherent at times. We were going to have to experiment a bit with his doses to find the best combination of morphine and ketamine.

He had one more pain crisis when they attempted to remove his Broviac with bedside sedation. The plan was to medicate him enough so that he wouldn't feel anything, but he would remain partially awake as they gently pulled out the tubing. It didn't work, and Chris screamed in pain. I made them stop and take him to surgery and put him completely out. I felt like I had let Chris down by allowing them to do the procedure that way. I should have known better.

It would have been easier to leave the Broviac in, but Chris was insistent. He wanted to spend his dying days being able to swim and sit in the hot tub. The hot tub had always been a great comfort to his aching body.

Chris would have to go home by ambulance, and the staff would have to coordinate the medications and necessary equipment with Hospice. We would take him home the next day. In the meantime, there were grim meetings with doctors and nurses to arrange the details.

It just so happened that the one doctor that we had had most conflict with regarding Chris's pain management was on duty that day. This particular doctor was fairly new, and hadn't known Chris the whole four years of his treatment; perhaps if she had, she may have battled us less when we had requested prescription refills.

So I regarded this one last meeting as an opportunity to make a lasting impression. "Doctor, you have let us down. I want you to remember my son, and all the times we begged you for pain pills that you thought weren't necessary. I want you to remember our Chris the next time you have a patient who tells you he's in pain."

I had tears in my eyes, and the doctor said very little. I hoped that I had reminded her to respect the fact that each patient is different, and that the pain control needs expressed by parents (who care for a chronically ill child for several years) should be taken more seriously.

I decided that if I were ever in charge of a pot of research money I would certainly conduct further studies in long-term pain management in children.

Having spoken my piece I made a conscious effort to try to let go of my anger. Aside from the pain issue I felt in my heart that Chris had received the best treatment possible. The doctors had done all that their limited earthly knowledge had allowed them to do.

And Chris continued to amaze us with his earthly humor.

July 2, 2001

... Chris did a little bit of his British accent this morning, "Would you like some tea and crumpets, dearie?" He said as the cafeteria worker wheeled the breakfast cart to the doorway. He was also doing his famous "ET" voice ... When Jem came in he called her "babe" and reminded her to call him "hubby." He was also talking a lot to himself, so Bobby jokingly asked him not to reveal any family secrets. "Don't worry, Dad," Chris replied, "I won't tell anyone you have a small penis."

Oh, God, Chris, how I'm going to miss you. No one else in the world has your sense of humor.

Along with that humor Chris displayed an incredible sense of peace and destiny. As I was packing up his room and I removed his schoolbooks from the shelf he said, "Well, Mom, I guess I won't be needing those anymore. Where I'm going, I won't need an education."

July 3, 2001 (Bob's entry)

I watched as Jem sat by Chris's bed. She let him hold her hand for a very long time. Chris gently caressed it, exploring her fingertips, and she never pulled away. I'm so glad she let him do that. It's the closest he'll ever come to having a girlfriend.

Nurse Nancy came up to me in the hallway that day. She had tears in her eyes as she handed me a Hershey's Kiss and said, "I'm so sorry."

Late that evening, around 11:00 PM the ambulance was finally ready and we left 2 Southwest for the very last time. Chris was stable, pain-free, and amazingly calm. Bobby, and Maureen and Al (who had come down to see Chris one more time) were driving home in separate cars. So when the paramedics gently lifted Chris out of his bed and onto the gurney I walked alone behind him. Everything seemed to be moving in slow motion, and the nurses' station was unusually quiet—no beeps, no phones ringing. 2 Southwest had been our island of safety for so long, now we were drifting away forever.

As we turned the corner and proceeded down the hall to the elevators I turned around one last time and silently flashed the nurses a peace sign.

Ambulances are supposed to take your child somewhere where they can make it all better. They aren't supposed to take your child home to die.

"You'll have to ride up front with the driver," one of the paramedics told me as they loaded Chris into the back.

"I'm riding with my son," I said firmly, climbing in behind Chris and giving the paramedic a look he didn't dare argue with.

Chris was serene. He spoke softly of how he wanted to go to the movies one more time before he went on to a better place. Yet, at the same time, the little boy still remained. "Mom, tell me when the ambulance gets to our neighborhood so you can ask the driver to blast the siren and flash the lights."

20

BEAUTY AND PAIN

Our house was filled with old people things—a wheelchair, a bedside commode, a portable oxygen pump, and boxes of medications. There should have been skateboards, roller blades, and dirty socks strewn about instead. Everything was backward—parents caring for their ailing son who now moved with the slow, ginger steps of the elderly.

Chris slept a lot, but when he was awake he was lucid and calm. We had to continuously increase his morphine, and occasionally his ketamine. The Hospice nurses and social workers were available to us twenty-four hours a day. They were warm and caring, but Chris liked his privacy, so after a few days, when we felt comfortable with the equipment, we told them that we didn't need them all the time. However, one nurse in particular was young and attractive, and Chris said, "She can stay."

I now understand how beauty and pain can exist side by side. There is nothing more painful than watching the decline of your child, and nothing more beautiful than witnessing his love and acceptance.

One day Bobby leaned over Chris's bed and said, "Buddy, I'm just not ready to lose you. I love you so much."

"Dad," he responded, "You have to let go. Jesus wants me, and when he calls, I'm going."

And so Chris became our guide and teacher. Clearly, he was already in touch with Heaven. "I know which angels are coming for me," he told us. "Jo Jo, Robert, and Michael."

As the days wore on, Chris slept more and more, but he continued to surprise us by suddenly becoming alert and responding to something we hadn't thought he'd heard. We had family all around, and Father John visited often. He asked Chris if he wanted to make his confirmation. It appeared that Chris slept through it, but the very next day he told Father John that he remembered.

Chris also made a special request to Bobby that week. "Dad," he said, "I'm going to give you the combination to my safe. There's a lot of money in there. I want you to use it to buy Jarrod and Erin the best birthday presents they ever had."

"Of course, buddy," Bobby had responded, choking back tears and in awe of Chris's selflessness.

Despite his weakened condition, Chris didn't want to use a catheter or a bed pan, so we would hoist him out of bed and into a wheelchair to go to the bathroom. He was no longer able to walk more than a few steps. Also, the morphine made it difficult for him to urinate, so the journeys to the bathroom often took more than a half hour.

He was the model patient. Like a small child, we had to help him in and out of his shorts, and hold him so he wouldn't topple. "Thank you," he'd say to us. "I don't know too many parents who would do all the things you do for me."

I remember crying and saying the same thing that I'd said to Chris many times before. "Chris, if I tried to imagine the most perfect son a mother could ever have, it doesn't even come close to the wonderful person you are. I am so lucky, that out of all the children in the world I got to be your mother."

Like most mothers, I have a unique and special relationship with each of my children, and love them with all of my heart, but Chris had always been my partner in crime. We shared the same sense of humor, and slightly off-center way of viewing the world. We had shared jokes and pranks that no one else thought was funny. I was losing my soul mate.

July 10, 2001

Now it's been more than a week since we brought Chris home to die. He continues to amaze us even in his weakened condition. Yesterday the Hospice nurse told us that he was slipping into a coma, and she started to insert a catheter. Suddenly Chris woke up and insisted on going to the bathroom ...

At night his breathing is ragged and harsh with periods of apnea. I guess that's what they call "the death rattle." Every time he stops breathing I think he has gasped his last breath. I lie on a mattress on the floor and drift in and out of a restless sleep, listening, waiting for his breathing to stop, but still daring to pray for a miracle ...

This week we signed a Do Not Resuscitate Order. That means if someone called paramedics they wouldn't do anything to prolong life. The Hospice nurses recommended that we sign it. I had mixed feelings, but I signed it. I actually signed a piece of paper that says not to save my son. I felt a little bit like I was betraying him, but in my heart, I know that they would only be attempting to resuscitate his body, not his soul. His soul is already saved.

That week we received one more gift of love from a very special family. This past year I had had the pleasure of teaching a delightful young lady named Ariel. Ariel was the kind of person who truly cared about the downtrodden. She played with the kids no one else wanted to. She helped the messy, disorganized boys clean out their desks and locate their long lost homework. Ariel always volunteered to be the partner to the ones with the greatest learning challenges, knowing full well that she would probably have to do more than her share of the work. And when I was up at the hospital Ariel always e-mailed me to ask how Chris was doing.

So the last time she e-mailed me I filled her in, and told her that we were bringing Chris home to die. When I read her response I was surprised to see a message from her father, JR, who owns a photography studio. He asked me to call him, and he requested the honor of coming to our home to do our family portrait.

"Chris can't sit up for more than ten minutes," I had warned him.

"Don't worry. I'll make it work, and it will be beautiful," JR had responded.

It was the last time Chris got out of bed. It took every ounce of strength that he had, and he knew perfectly well that it was the last picture that would ever be taken of him. When JR called us later to tell us the portrait was ready he told us that Chris had smiled in every single pose. Ariel's family's gift and Chris's final act of love and courage had provided us with a photograph that we would treasure forever. In the picture, Chris sits in the center as if to hold us all together.

After the picture Chris wanted to move to the sofa out in the family room. He wanted to be in the center of the activity. He would remain a social being to the very end.

July 10, 2001 cont'd

Father John couldn't come today so he called Chris and asked him how he was doing. Chris said, "Good." Imagine that—he said, "good." I guess that would be a gross exaggeration in earthly terms, but a fairly accurate statement for someone about to experience the joy of Heaven.

At this point Chris could not speak above a whisper. When he had something to say we would lean over, desperate for every word. His last words to us were

"I'll be a guardian angel for the whole family. When I'm in Heaven you can look up and talk to me and I'll hear you. I love you."

At 8:30 in the morning on July twelfth Christopher Robert Ditmars took his last breath. His last breath was really an exhalation, his body expelling the pain and disease and sending his wonderful soul Heavenward.

Chris had given us the greatest gift that a child can bestow upon his parents. He had thanked us for taking care of him, he had told us that he loved us, and he had reassured us that he would be OK.

21

A FEATHER UNDER MY PILLOW

Other people who have lost loved ones had told us that we would feel numb for a while. Some told us that Chris would give us strength. Many said that they could not even begin to imagine our pain. They were all right. And on the day that we laid Chris to rest they all came, hundreds of them.

Our church holds over twelve hundred, and it was nearly full. Chris had managed to bring the community together one last time. "Well, Chris did it again," Father John said to us at the beginning of the mass. "Bishop Nevins is here. He heard about Chris on the news, and he felt that he needed to be here."

Chris had made such an impact on the community that two news channels ran a story about his death. His obituary had a photo and ran three columns. Our intense grief was tempered with immense pride. We could not have been prouder if Chris had won a Nobel Peace Prize.

Every teacher that had ever taught Chris came, and they told us what an effect he'd had on their lives. Even the Superintendent of Schools was there. We were the parents of a hero.

But as we followed the casket slowly up the aisle to the altar, Bobby and Jarrod looking dashing in their black tuxedos, Erin and I in our finest dresses, I felt more like a lost soul than the mother of a hero. It was the last time the Ditmars, family of five, would be physically present in the church.

Although I have trouble remembering much of what was said, each person that spoke at the funeral mass captured beautifully the different aspects of Chris's personality. Father John spoke of Chris's spiritual strength, and the incredible peace that surrounded him in the end. Uncle Al shared amusing anecdotes about Chris and spoke of the great value that Chris placed on human relationships. Former teachers praised Chris as a hero, and told of lessons that he had taught them. Bobby and I somehow found the strength to stand up and read our special letter to our angel that we had written, but I think it was Dr. Marilyn Highland (Bay Haven principal) who said it best. "All along we kept praying for a miracle," she said. "But then I realized that Chris *was* the miracle."

I knew that we would have a roller coaster of grief and gut-wrenching sorrow ahead of us. Christopher's journey on Earth was over, and ours was just beginning. I prayed to him to be our guide.

Chris,
Our love is endless and forever.
It is not bound by the limits of time, space,
Or Earthly mortality.
Chris.

In one of their very last conversations Bobby had asked Chris to send us a sign that he was OK. Chris asked his father to pick the sign and Bobby had chosen a feather. "How about putting a feather under my pillow, buddy?" Bob had requested.

Chris responded to this request with the same humor and compassion he had exhibited in his short, powerful life. Three days after the funeral Bobby and I awoke to find dozens of goose down feathers scattered in our bed. Not the tiny wisps that sometimes leak out when changing linens, but full-sized feathers. "Have our down pillows sprung a leak?" We asked ourselves. We removed the pillowcases and turned the pillows over and over, but couldn't find a hole. Still pondering this amazing occurrence I walked into the bathroom and glanced at my reflection in the mirror. There on my right shoulder rested a tiny, perfect little feather. It was almost as if it had drifted down amid the joyous commotion of Jo Jo, Robert, and Michael high-fiving Heaven's newest angel.

Epilogue: Letters to Chris

* Note: These are the letters written in the journal that I left at the hospital. Later, I passed it around Bay Haven.

7/4/01

Dear Family,

My memories of Chris and the family go back as far as I've worked at All Children's Hospital. He was one of the first patients I worked with. I remember playing PICTIONARY over and over through all of his relapses. I especially remember when Chris drew the word "playboy" and drew this: (a stick figure with breasts) for me to guess. Needless to say that was hilarious!

Now on to Video bingo. I could always count on prank calls from Chris. My favorites were "the pizza delivery guy" or the "Chinese food delivery guy." And your bingo earrings, Maribeth.... the time you all brought the fart machine to video bingo it lasted two hours because I laughed so much! Another funny memory is when we took a bunch of donated animal pictures, cut their heads off and put them on different bodies ... we had Doberman heads on little poodles. And probably my best memory was the time we went for a walk and Chris told me about his motor scooter and how fast it went. That reminded me that Chris was just like any other kid and that's why it's my favorite. I will really miss you, Chris. The last thing you told me was "I'll try," and did you ever. I hope you get your driver's license in Heaven.

Ethan S., Child-life Therapist, ACH

Dear Family of My Husband Chris,

I remember the first time I met Chris—I really didn't know how to take him. But from that first time I met him he had my heart. Chris was always snuggled in his homemade blankets looking just as cozy as possible. I then found out that I had something in common with the family—I run marathons. I will be running the marathon at Disney World on January 6, 2002 and will do it in his memory ... The last visits before Chris left to go home we spent a lot of time together and I really got to know what a wonderful, grown up person he is. He told me that he wasn't scared to die and that he would be a spirit for his parents and big sis, but he would be a guardian angel for his little brother because he's going to need help. He then told me how he was going to divide all of his things and who he was going to give them to. He talked so calm and cool and every time I needed to leave he begged me to stay, so I did and we talked some more. He then decided he wanted me to call him 'honey' and that he would call me 'baby'. So it was decided that we would now have pet names. A few days later my name for him changed to 'hubby'—this made him very happy, and to see him smile made me happy. Chris, like a lot of the other kids here you taught me to reach for the sky and not to be afraid of anything—make every day special. Chris, you will always be in my thoughts and forever in my heart.

Love Always, Jemma

Chris,

Perhaps it is funny that the first thing that I recall about you is that I taught you the art of making water guns out of syringes. Perhaps it is very appropriate. I have learned that you and your family are able to have fun and live life to its fullest in times and places that could be seen as impossible to do so. You have laughed on a cancer ward—dressed as doctors at Halloween parties—made toys out of things that many people associate with pain (water guns from syringes!) So my friends, I am sad that you have gone home without the cure we all hoped for you. But I pray that you will continue to live life to its fullest and know that we have learned—I have learned much from your spirit. My God bless you and keep you.

Paul B., Chaplain, ACH

Dear Family,

When I think of Chris Ditmars I think of laughing, smiling, joking, and honesty. I will always remember the walks we would take where Chris wanted to tell me about his dreams of someday being a Child-life Therapist. Chris said he would make a great one because he could tell the kids just how things will happen and how they would feel because he had experienced everything himself.

I also remember one day when Chris called me as I walked by his room and he acted like he vomited on his table. I ran to grab towels and he started to laugh as he showed me the fake vomit he had brought from home. He got me good!!

… Chris, I wish you peace, NO PAIN, and only comfort! Chris, you asked me if I thought you could drive in heaven? I know that you will drive the coolest and fastest car in heaven!! Thank you for letting me be a part of your family's journey. I have learned so much from the Ditmars.

Love Kim Daugherty, Child-life Therapist ACH

Dear Chris,

Where to start? We all go back so far. I remember when you first came to us you were so sweet, and then some nurse taught you about silly string and squirting water with syringes. Whenever I was your nurse I knew going into your room I would usually come out covered with something! I always had fun with you. Your mother's earrings have made a big impression on me also. Chris, I admire your bravery for fighting this leukemia that you have had to battle. Whenever I go to heaven I will expect you to be waiting for me with sticky, smelly, silly string.

Love, Nurse Nancy

Dear Chris and family,

How or why you all are so very deep in my heart I may never know. I do know you will be there always. My memories of you will be happy ones: the Spaghettio's you loved so much, the day your dad tried to look as cool as you with his shaved hair cut, and the strength I could see in your eyes the very first time I saw you. My heart will be sad missing you, but in my soul your happy smile will stay forever.

Love, Carla (AKA Ronald McDonald House Mom)

Dear Chris and Family,

When I started at Ronald McDonald House all I heard about was this awesome family—The Ditmars! It's true, they are very special, but that Chris is AWE-SOME!

... I always wanted to make sure he was eating properly ... I would always take him or give him the key to go down to the dungeon and select his favorite cans of food—Spaghettio's and ravioli ... If he had wanted a steak I would have found a way.

Chris was the featured "star" at the RMH luncheon this year while Maribeth was the featured speaker. You are a star in everyone's life that you have touched, Chris. When I look up and see that bright sparkle in the sky I'll say "Hi Chris." I'm honored to know you.

Sally Jo at RMH West

Dear Chris and Family (including Ollie Klump!)

Chris, I want to take this special opportunity to tell you that I grew to love you through the wonderful stories told to me by your family. You were in the hospital so much—we didn't have a lot of one to one conversations. I could tell that we would have been the best of buds because I love your great sense of humor. Please visit us at RMH after you 'cross over'—we'll be watching for your sign! (Nothing real weird, though, please!)

... You all became our "special" family, part of our lives and part of the RMH household ... I will always think about your strengths, patience, and awesome attitudes.

Love, Judy Glass, RMH West Manager

Dear Ditmars Family,

It is with such a heavy heart that I write this today, having just heard that Chris has passed away ... I want to thank you for allowing us to be part of this journey you have been on. You have shared with us so many thoughts and feelings that will help us to reach out and help others with a hug, a kind word, or a smile. You took the time to come and share your story with the volunteers at the brunch and to tell the public about your stays at RMH during the telethon ...

... You will always be a part of our extended family (and our arms are wide!) Together we will get through these tough times as we remember Chris with love.

Fondly, Donna RMH

To the Ditmars,

I feel like I have known you guys forever and it seems so strange not to have you here now. Even in the toughest times you guys had your sense of humor and made this sad and sometimes scary place a unit full of laughter and a little more bearable. Chris was an amazing kid and very brave, even to the end. I'm sure it must be hard now to be home and make the separation. You probably have lost touch of what normal people do from day to day when they don't have a chronically ill child to care for. I remember you guys as a very active family who traveled a lot and I hope you continue to do all of those things and keep Chris with you in spirit ... Chris will always be my inspiration of bravery when I talk to new families embarking on your journey.

Love, Nareda, nurse ACH

Dear Ditmars Family,

... I will always remember Chris as being a joker and a prankster ... from that first time when red dye was put into the urine to the time I had to sing and dance the Will Smith song "Welcome to Miami" And that is how I will remember Chris ... My heart, thoughts, and prayers go out to you guys.

Lots of Love, Maria, Nurse ACH

Dear Chris and Family,

I always enjoyed taking care of Chris—he was always very easy-going and made my job easier and was never demanding. I enjoyed him when he would play jokes on other nurses, especially getting Nancy wet! Chris was a very intelligent kid. He made things easy when explaining procedures to him. He fascinated me with the way he took pills ... I am grateful for having the opportunity of knowing such a special person like Chris. He touched every person he met in so many different ways. He will live on in our memories.

My thoughts are With You,

Mary Ann, Nurse, ACH

Dear Family,

Over the past two years I have had both the honor and pleasure of taking care of Chris many times. One of my fondest memories of Chris was the time he was pretending to be asleep in his room while he and his roommate made noises with the "fart machine" every time I walked into the room. No matter how much I tried to deny it, he and his roomie had a ball telling everyone else who entered the room all about my "flatulence problem." It makes me smile and laugh even as I write this letter. But this is a perfect example of how I will remember Chris; smiling, laughing, playing pranks ... so brave going through everything that he had to endure. Chris, Mom, and your whole family will remain in my thoughts and prayers.

God Bless, Inez S., nurse ACH

The Ditmars!

Fun, Fun, Fun!!!! Look out for the poop! I remember the (rubber) poop on the floor in the nurses' station ... never a dull moment when you had Chris as your patient ... This is truly a loss for everyone who knew and loved him. I hope that knowing Chris touched so many people in a positive way will somehow help you. I believe that Chris will always be part of this place with no pain, no chemo, and no sickness—only good memories. One last thought: LOOK OUT, HEAVEN! (Any fart machines up there?)

Paula, RN, clinic

Ditmars Family,

... I always loved the days when Chris came to the clinic because he'd always mess with the screen saver to say silly things—usually it was "Chris Ditmars is #1," Well, Chris you are #1. Thank you for sharing your laughter with me.

Jane W, RN

To the very Special Ditmars Family!

... ROCK camp has never been the same. I was looking at some old photo albums and so much has changed. You grew both physically and spiritually as well. You have all been a wonderful support for Chris, each other, and other families ... Your family will be missed in our lives. My thoughts and prayers are with you.

Nurse Ellen

Maribeth and Bob,

Wanting—wishing—wondering—unreal—but real. Questioning—learning.

You have withstood a living hell and walked through fire because of your intense and all consuming love for your son, Chris. You did your very, very best to save your son. And when that wasn't possible you helped him face his death with dignity and humor and openness ... He loved you so much.

Lynda Walker, Social Worker

All the Ditmars (including Chris),

... When it came to schoolwork Chris's personality would be an extra bonus to otherwise dull assignments. Thus the famous "elephant poop" story. Chris managed to write about 30 sentences using vocabulary words correctly but always with the words 'elephant poop' worked into the sentence. What's even worse he talked me into scribing for him so I actually had to write those words. Needless to say, I'll never see the words (or the actual) elephant poop again without remembering this story.

... Chris and his family shared themselves with those around them despite their own private ordeal ... You have touched my life in countless ways. I will miss the physical presence of the Ditmars at ACH, but will always have your spirits in my heart ...

Gail the teacher
8/18/01

When I think of Chris, I smile. He brought tremendous joy into my life. Being his schoolteacher and homebound teacher in fifth grade were special experiences I will cherish always. My time with Chris was a blessing to me ... He was the first student to utilize my pig mailbox by sending me a note ... whenever he came to visit he always left me a note ... he responded to my puns and jokes and laughed even when no one else did; he helped me teach two entire homeroom classes about courage and compassion ... After a homebound session when he was feeling pretty perky he taught me how to ride his scooter ... The last time I saw Chris was at the end of this school year (2001) when he and Maribeth came for a brief visit ... we had our picture taken together ... Chris wandered around the classroom. I think he was collecting memories.

The day of Chris's memorial I was on the beach in Ocean City, Maryland. There were butterflies everywhere, flitting here or there. One or more would occasionally land on me for a brief stay. No other day that week were there any butterflies on the beach.

With much love,
Ms. Jane Keil

August 20, 2001

Dearest Chris,

I am looking at your picture—the one on all those flyers for your blood drive in April. We all had such high hopes for a match for you. What a turnout! I've never seen such community support for anything. So many people loved you. I can still see your dad with his head shaved to look like you. (Actually, you looked just like him!)

... In my math class you were bright, sweet, and your smile lit up the whole room ... My daughter Karen was inspired to collect gifts for you through her National Honor Society. So many teens were inspired ... to participate. On St.

Patrick's Day we delivered the gifts (to the hospital). It will always be the best St. Patrick's Day of my life—seeing you with your bald painted head and your mom painting shamrocks on everything in sight. You immediately assembled several sets of Legos (You'd have been a gifted engineer).

In June when I delivered some gifts from my class to your house, that was the last time I saw you. I sent cards as often as possible, and Chris, to this day I can't walk into a store without being drawn to the cards for you. I really miss that part of my life.

My daughter Christina accompanied me to your memorial service … like so many she was touched by you. She found out about the "Light the Night" walk on Siesta Key for the Leukemia and Lymphoma Society … Christina asked her babysitting customers this summer to donate her fee to the cause …

Dear Chris you are like a pebble tossed into a pond. It creates ripples in ever-widening rings. Your life continues to cause a rippling effect. Your presence will be felt for so long, and in more ways than you or your family could ever imagine.

I wish you peace, and through yours, peace for your loving, devoted family.

Love, Mrs. Fenton, Bay Haven teacher

8/22/01

… At first Chris was very quiet, but whenever I heard an unusual sound outside in the parking lot or in the hallway, I could almost predict after a while that it was "you know who"! Once when Chris presented a book project he used his gerbil as the character Ralph S. Mouse from the book, The Mouse and The Motorcycle! To coin an old phrase he was always thinking "outside the box."

Chris also was earning class store (a reward for good behavior) during our Fun Fridays so it shouldn't have surprised me that when I went to a party at his house during the summer I discovered the contents of our home (items donated to the class store) throughout Chris's home … candles, artificial flowers, kitchen knick-knacks, etc. It was a riot to discover that truly "One man's junk is another man's treasure!" However, there's one special item that I hold near and dear to me, and that's a teacher gift of a teddy bear in a graduation cup (that also holds pencils) made of ceramic and resin that Chris gave me when he graduated from fifth grade. Every time I need a pencil or a pen, I'm continually reminded of how much I need Chris to teach me how precious the little moments that make up a lifetime are … I hope you are looking down on planet earth so I can show you the impact you've made in my classroom and my life.

Love, MaryAlice Hratko, varying exceptionalities teacher, Bay Haven

---

My Most Memorable Moment of Chris Ditmars!

My most memorable moment of Chris Ditmars was when I had first started working at Bay Haven and I was walking past Cass Bowman's room. All of a sudden this very cute and sweet freckled face second grade boy came skipping out of the room and handed me a little chocolate heart and said "HAPPY VALENTINE'S DAY, MRS. HUBBARD!"

Linda Hubbard, technology aide, Bay Haven

August 28, 2001

Dear Chris,

I miss you! Please know how sad I am that you had to leave us so soon. Your strength, your courage, and your amazing sense of humor were far greater than anybody I have ever known. As I rubbed your head each time I saw you, my wishes for you were to feel at peace.

A favorite memory of you will always be of you acting as the Basics Plus D.J. for our jogathon. You were fabulous! You took charge. You handled the music, you shared your "Whassup" in your special Chris voice, and you cheered for all the joggers. You related so well to all the children and you handled each child's request for the next song with the famous Chris diplomacy and a grin. You did an incredible job!

You are in your new home now with a new set of friends and I have no doubts that you are touching them as you touched all of us. I look forward to seeing you again when it is my turn to move on. In the meantime, I promise to give my support and my love to your mom, dad, sister, and brother.

Love,

Dr. Marilyn Highland, principal, Bay Haven Basics Plus

Dear Chris,

When I think of you, great memories, laughter, and a boy with a whole lot of courage come to mind. Whenever people talk about angels, I feel like they're talking about you! You really changed my life. I looked at you and said to myself, "That boy is so strong!" ... I pray for you asking God to let you know that I'll always remember you.

Love, Emma (fifth grade classmate)

P.S. I made this bracelet and wore it when my mom told me that you had passed away. It is my small gift to your family. (The bracelet has beads that read "Chris is forever.")

Dear Chris,

My first memory of you is of you swinging by your legs upside down in the banyan tree outside portable 1. "Who is this child and how dare he?!" Then you looked up and grinned—your mom's impish grin—and I knew who you were.

I came to love that grin, Chris—when you'd wear it coming into my classroom for math ... And ... later your mom would describe your latest hospital antic, I could imagine the two of you grinning from ear to ear as you plagued the hospital staff with your stunts.

Your mom has been wearing angel earrings the last few times I saw her. I like to imagine they are both grinning—one for you and one for her.

Love, Connie O'Gorman, Bay Haven teacher

Dearest Chris and Family,

... I admired all of you so very much, and frequently felt helpless to alleviate the depths of your journey through truly horrific times. My dad died from leukemia, and though it was about twenty years ago he is still with me. Just as you will be with your family for now and forever. God bless all of you, may he put his loving arms around you and hold you dearly.

Love Peggy Atkinson, Bay Haven teacher

September 8, 2001

Dear Chris,

I remember when you were in Mrs. Bowman's class in second grade … You would hide under the computer stand unbeknownst to me so that when I arrived and couldn't find you I'd walk all the way back upstairs to Mrs. Bowman's room … I'd go back and forth and look in the bathroom and so forth. Finally I'd hear a giggle … I kept special treats in my refrigerator that belonged to me. You never wanted the snacks that I gave out … Sure enough you'd talk me into giving you some candy that I only give to my special friends … Do you also remember when I kept telling you to come down out of that tree? You always replied, "My mom knows I'm in this tree!" … Now you're hiding in heaven and eating lots of candy and climbing trees galore! Alleluia! Amen!

Love Always,

Annette Humphrey, teacher's aide, Bay Haven

Dear Chris,

Your smiling face is greatly missed around school, but the wonderful impact you have had on our lives will be with us forever.

… You were always excited about everything we did and you were ready to dive into every new experience … Even when you left second grade I cherish the many times you would come into my room checking out what was in the school store, wanting to borrow the gerbil ball, or wanting to help me. I enjoy the time you helped me be a leprechaun. You put footprints and glitter all over. Your love for fun had you borrow the paint and glitter so you could bring the leprechauns to Jarrod. I also remember when you were our disc jockey at our jog. You have always brought your zest for love and life to everyone …

I do healing at my church and I can truly feel your presence. I guess you can help a lot more people from heaven … and I know I can feel you helping them.

… You have touched my life and have left beautiful footprints on my heart that will stay with me always.

Love You Much,

Cass Bowman

Dear Chris and Family,

When I think of Chris I remember the big tree outside the lunchroom. He loved to play in that tree. He would call my name and then try to hide from me. And I remember he loved his chocolate milk and his nutty buddies.

But what will stay with me always is his smile and his unbelievable strength.

Love You!

Joanne, lunchroom supervisor, Bay Haven

Dear Chris, Bob, Maribeth, Erin, Jarrod,

Relationships are a great source of amazement.... Experiencing the dynamic flow of give and take, finding joy and laughing despite the circumstances, feeling a deep connection, feeling content just to be in each other's presence: this is the beauty of relationship ... I feel very fortunate that I was one of the people with whom Chris chose to have a close, special relationship ... Despite the decades of age difference there was a deep recognition that we had something to give each other.

... During one of my family's annual visits to Florida ... Chris had planned a night out with Uncle "Owl" ... he had arranged for us to have Erin's convertible Mustang. Of course we cruised with the top down. We started at Applebee's sitting at the high tables near the bar. We of course took stock of the best looking waitresses. Before we departed a few choice spitballs had to be shot at unwary, nearby patrons. We made a speedy exit to Chris's favorite haunt, the $1.50 movie theater ... Afterwards, thanks to the steroids he was on, Chris was hungry again and we went to Taco Bell. I used Fisher Steven's Asian-Indian accent from the movie "Short Circuit" when I ordered ... We both laughed a lot. At one point Chris was laughing so hard his chaloopa passed through his nose ... it was after midnight and our escapades weren't over. We went to the 24 hour Wal-Mart and bought a battery operated plane ... On its maiden flight the plane landed on the neighbor's roof ...

... Despite my 43 years there is inside me a 14-year-old boy who never quite got over the loss of his Nana in 1971. It was as if my youthful joy was lost ... suspended in time. The gift I received from a 14-year-old boy who matured to a young man before his time, who faced death with acceptance and dignity ... the gift I received was to reclaim my youthful joy lost some 30 years ago. An adult acting like a child, a child forced to mature to a man. I know I received what I needed from Chris. I trust Chris received what he needed from all those he gave so much too.

Love,

Uncle Al

Dear Chris, Maribeth, Bob, Erin, and Jarrod,

It's hard to put into words how one young person can have such an impact on so many lives ... When life gets challenging, I think of you in your short 14 years, and how courageous you were. I think of you lying in your hospital bed, feeling lousy, and asking <u>me</u> how I am! You are missed more than you'll ever know, Chris. But you'll live long in my heart and in the hearts of so many others. One of the last things you said to me was, "Aunt Maureen, I love you so much." I love you, too, Chris, and I thank you for being the very special young man you were, and for being the very special angel you are. I know your family has a huge hole in their hearts right now ... but I pray that someday the pain may subside and they will really come to know how blessed we all were to have you with us—even if for a very short period of time.

Love Always, Aunt Maureen

Dear Chris,

Your stay on this planet was much too short, but my memories of you will never die. When I visited you in Florida I always took you to the theme parks. I remember one time, as we were driving to the Magic Kingdom, we saw a woman get pulled over for speeding. When you asked me what was going on I explained that she was getting a ticket, and you asked, "A ticket to Disney World?"

We always had a ball! On Space Mountain I was somewhat terrified, but you weren't. I opted out from Big Thunder Mountain Railroad, but you were ready for anything. The rides at Universal Studios were hairy, scary, and contrary, but nothing scared you!

Chris, you are now in a better place with your friends like Jo Jo. God bless you always, Chris. I love you, I've always loved you, and I will always love you.

Till we meet again,

Uncle Jim Parisho

Dear Bob and Maribeth,

My thoughts and prayers are with you and your family with the loss of Chris. Chris was an outstanding witness to life itself. He was a young man with an 'old' soul, filled with spiritual strength, not only for himself, but for others. When Chris died God's name was blessed and heaven rejoiced. Although he died young, he remains a constant reminder of how we are to live and cope with life.

Chris could not have had better parents. Bob and Maribeth your love and devotion for Chris has imprinted a perpetual image on my mind and soul what parenting is all about.

I do believe that we will be with Chris in the kingdom—there he'll greet us all with laughter, energy, and fun. He promised that he would watch over you both (so you better behave yourselves) and that will be the greatest gift of all.

With God's love and peace,

Father John

A LETTER TO OUR ANGEL
MONDAY, JULY 16, 2001

Dear Chris,

You are an angel that we borrowed for a little while. While you were here you taught us so many things—most of them were about living, but some of our lessons were also about dying.

You taught us to appreciate everything: family closeness, and special times together. "Mom, sit down," you'd say, "Let's make soft pretzels and watch a movie together." Or, "Dad, how about just you and me go to The Salty Dog for a cup of clam chowder?"

You didn't roll your eyes and act embarrassed to be around us like most teenagers. Instead, you let us hold your hand, and every day you told us that you loved us.

You showed us how to endure hardship with such humor and vitality. You had silly nicknames for all of us. The nurses at All Children's were Smurf, Babe, Reindeer, and Smelly Melly. Mom was Mommy Meatball, and Dad was Daddio Spaghettio or 'Da-Spa-ga' for short. Sometimes you drove the hospital staff nuts with your antics. We had fabulous water fights and silly string battles. One time you started an all out water war on 2 southwest. Armed with syringes full of water we all crouched on either side of the nurses' station and blasted away. Remember Nurse Nancy didn't have anything to shoot with, so she chased us all the way down the hallway with a cup of water. Then someone said, "Oh no, the supervisor's coming," so we all made a mad dash for towels to mop up the floor!

Chris, we loved your impersonations and funny voices. You could imitate all sorts of foreign accents and cartoon characters. You used to make prank calls from your hospital bed to the child-life extension during their video bingo games. You'd pretend to have the wrong number and try to order a pizza, or you'd speak in your ET alien voice. We'd watch the TV monitor and laugh when they'd say, "We know that's you, Chris!"

But, sadly, there were many times when you were too sick to play, especially this last year of treatment. You endured bone wracking pain and blistering mouth sores. Still, you rarely complained. Your pity parties never lasted more than 10 minutes. Instead you'd speak softly of better days ahead—days when you'd play soccer again, grow hair, get your 6 pack back, and as you put it, no longer be "butt ugly". Sometimes you'd have visitors when you were too sick to carry on a conversation. We'd ask you if you wanted them to leave, and you'd open your eyes just long enough to say, "No, tell everyone to just sit around me and have regular conversations."

Chris, you taught us about heaven. You saw some of your buddies in the hospital die, and quickly learned to face adult issues. When your friend Jo Jo died you told us that he was in heaven playing Frisbee with our deceased dog, Moonshine. "But now," you explained, "Moonshine has finally learned how to catch the Frisbee." Chris, you also enabled us to glimpse a little bit of heaven in the many acts of kindness and generosity that we have received from our community. For every medical setback you experienced, countless people came forward with prayers, gifts, and favors. You brought out the love in everyone around you.

It was less than 3 weeks ago that you found out you were terminal. That very same day you asked nurse Jem to hurry up and marry you, and you made her call you "hubby" whenever she entered your room. "Don't cry, Mom and Dad," you said, "I'm going to a better place." You promised to be our guardian angel and always watch over us. "You're going to need the help with Jarrod," you added.

Chris, you also taught the Sarasota community about the gift of life. You brought us all together and reminded us how a simple blood test can save a life. You, and Erin, and Jarrod, attended boring banquets and listened to long speeches. We knew you were tired, and that you'd rather be in your room building Legos or playing video games. For so many you put a face on cancer research, a face that all of us will never forget.

Chris, you were just a little boy when you were diagnosed with leukemia four years ago, but you died a young man much wiser than your 14 years. One of the very last things you ever said to us was simply a whispered "Thank you." How many parents of teenagers ever get to hear that? Well, now we are the parents of an angel, and we say to you, Chris, "Thank you."

Love Forever,

Mom and Dad

THE MOONPUPPY SONG
(With apologies to Cat Stevens)

Chorus:

I'm being followed by a Moonpuppy, Moonpuppy, Moonpuppy

Leap'in and hopp'in with a Moonpuppy, Moonpuppy, Moonpuppy

Verse 1:

If I throw him a bone

He won't beg, he won't moan

If I throw him a bone

Waaaag, Waaag, Waaag his tail

Repeat Chorus

Verse 2:

If I throw him a Frisbee

He will run and He'll be free

If I throw him a Frisbee

Waaaag, Waaag, Waaaag his tail

Repeat chorus

Verse 3:

If I take him for a walk

He will pounce and he will stalk

If I take him for a walk

Waaag, Waaag, Waaag his tail

Repeat chorus

Verse 4:

If I take him for a run

He will bark and he'll have fun

If I take him for a run

Waaaag, Waaag, Waaaag his tail

Repeat chorus

Verse 5:

If I take him for a walk

Maybe he will learn to talk

If I take him for a walk

Waaaag, Waaag, Waaaag his tail
Repeat Chorus

Songs of Love Foundation
Words and Music by Danny Obadia
Vocals and Rap by Danny Obadia

Chris Ditmars

There's only one thing on my wish list
To spend some time with Chris
'Cause Chris Ditmars he's the man
Listen close I'm gonna tell you this
There's no one in the world quite like Chris
Chris Ditmars yea he's the man

This song's going out to my man Chris
So listen close I don't want you to miss
All the great things that he's all about
It will make you proud
Chris Ditmars he does it all
Snowboarding, Playstation, hockey, football
His athletic skills are beyond compare
Take him on if you dare
There he goes on his go-ped he's like a blur
When he's on the move just call him sir
He can fly like a bird all day long
Into the night he's still going strong
And on the soccer field he can score at will
You'll be amazed at his awesome skill
He's a leader, a winner, he's not a quitter
He's got more assets than Dean Witter …

With Bugsy and Gizmo his four-legged friends
He always has a blast the fun never ends

They love Chris it's easy to tell
They've got a strong bond that's as clear as a bell
Chris and Jarrod play all the time
When they're together everything is fine
Going to the movies and listening to rap
They're a barrel of laughs you can count on that
The family vacation is his favorite of all
That's when Chris really has a ball
A nice cruise ship a big ocean liner
Chris Ditmars knows there's nothing finer
One day soon when he's a famous young man
He'll take his friends on a cruise from here to Japan
He's the life of the party he's going far
The one and only Chris Ditmars ...

978-1-58348-937-6
1-58348-937-1

CPSIA information can be obtained
at www.ICGtesting.com
Printed in the USA
FFOW02n0236050418
46159486-47360FF